ALSO BY HAROLD BLOOM

SHAKESPEARE'S PERSONALITIES

LEAR

THE GREAT IMAGE
OF AUTHORITY

HAROLD BLOOM

SCRIBNER

New York   London   Toronto   Sydney   New Delhi

Scribner
An Imprint of Simon & Schuster, Inc.
1230 Avenue of the Americas
New York, NY 10020

First Scribner trade paperback edition April 2019

SCRIBNER and design are registered trademarks of The Gale Group, Inc.,
used under license by Simon & Schuster, Inc., the publisher of this work.

For information about special discounts for bulk purchases,
please contact Simon & Schuster Special Sales at 1-866-506-1949
or business@simonandschuster.com.

The Simon & Schuster Speakers Bureau can bring authors to your live event.
For more information or to book an event, contact the Simon & Schuster Speakers
Bureau at 1-866-248-3049 or visit our website at www.simonspeakers.com.

Interior design by Erich Hobbing

Manufactured in the United States of America

3   5   7   9   10   8   6   4   2

The Library of Congress has cataloged the hardcover edition as follows:

Names: Bloom, Harold, author.
Title: Lear : the great image of authority / Harold Bloom.
Description: First Scribner hardcover edition. | New York : Scribner, 2018. |
Series: Shakespeare's personalities | Includes bibliographical references and index.
Identifiers: LCCN 2017061767 (print) | LCCN 2018000054 (ebook) | ISBN
9781501164217 (ebook) | ISBN 9781501164194 (hardback)
Subjects: LCSH: Lear, King of England (Legendary character) | Shakespeare,
William, 1564–1616. King Lear. | Kings and rulers in literature. | BISAC:
LITERARY CRITICISM / Shakespeare. | LITERARY CRITICISM / Renaissance. |
LITERARY CRITICISM / Drama.
Classification: LCC PR2993.L4 (ebook) | LCC PR2993.L4 B57 2018 (print) | DDC
822.3/3—dc23
LC record available at https://lccn.loc.gov/2017061767

ISBN 978-1-5011-6419-4
ISBN 978-1-5011-6420-0 (pbk)
ISBN 978-1-5011-6421-7 (ebook)

For Susan Spero and
Gary Heller

Contents

CONTENTS

Acknowledgments

I would like to acknowledge my remarkable research assistant, Alice Kenney, and my devoted editor, Nan Graham. As always I am indebted to my literary agents, Glen Hartley and Lynn Chu. I have a particular debt to Glen Hartley, who first suggested this sequence of five brief books on Shakespeare's personalities.

Author's Note

In the main, I have followed the 1997 Arden edition, but have repunctuated according to my understanding of the text. In a few places, I have restored Shakespeare's language, where I judge traditional emendations to be mistaken.

LEAR

THE GREAT IMAGE OF AUTHORITY

CHAPTER 1

Every Inch a King

Shakespeare's most challenging personalities are Prince Hamlet and King Lear. *The Tragedy of Hamlet Prince of Denmark* and *The Tragedy of King Lear* rival each other as the two ultimate dramas yet conceived by humankind.

Hamlet and Lear have virtually nothing in common. The Prince of Denmark carries intellect and consciousness to their limits. King Lear of Britain lacks self-awareness and any understanding of other selves, yet his capacity for feeling is beyond measure.

The ironies of both personalities are too large to be fully seen. Readers and playgoers have to confront the difficulty of judging what is ironic and what is not. Hamlet's inwardness is available to us through his seven soliloquies but their interpretation frequently is blocked because no other dramatic protagonist is so adept at not saying what he means or not meaning what he says. Lear incessantly proclaims his anguish, fury, outrage, and grief, and while he means everything he says, we never become accustomed to his amazing range of intense feeling. His violent expressionism desires us to experience his inmost being, but we lack the resources to receive that increasing chaos.

We know almost nothing of Shakespeare's own inwardness. His beliefs or absence of them cannot be induced from his plays or poems. I find it useless to speculate about his religious orientation.

Whether Shakespeare the man was Protestant or recusant Catholic, skeptic or nihilist, I neither know nor care. *Hamlet* and *King Lear* both contain biblical references but neither is a "Christian" drama. There is no question of redemption in either play. A Christian work, however tragic, must finally be optimistic.

In *King Lear* there are only three survivors: Edgar, Albany, Kent. Lear and Gloucester die of inextricably fused joy and grief. The monsters Goneril, Regan, Cornwall, Oswald all die violently. Edmund the Bastard is cut down by his half brother Edgar. The Fool vanishes. Cordelia is murdered. When Lear dies, there are apocalyptic overtones:

> Kent: Is this the promised end?
> Edgar: Or image of that horror?
> Albany: Fall, and cease.
>
> act 5, scene 3, lines 261–62

Those are not the accents of Christian optimism. Shakespeare being Shakespeare, I have not the temerity to suggest precisely what they are. The gods of *King Lear* are curiously Roman in name though the more or less historical King Leir was supposed to have reigned about the time of the founding of Rome, in the eighth century before the Common Era. That might have made Leir the contemporary of the prophet Elijah, and so alive a century before King Solomon the Wise.

King James I, who was the crucial member of the audience attending Shakespeare's plays from 1603 until 1613, has been called "the wisest fool in Christendom." As King he regarded himself as a mortal God and fancied he was the new King Solomon. He is perhaps the only monarch of Britain who was an intellectual of sorts, and he wrote a few mediocre books. His clashes with Parliament over revenues foreshadowed the disaster of his son and successor Charles I, beheaded for high treason in January 1649.

When Lear speaks of the great image of authority, his bitterness bursts forth: "a dog's obeyed in office." Yet Kent, the loyal follower whom he has exiled, and who disguises himself so as to go on serving Lear, seeks and finds authority in the great King:

> **Lear:** What art thou?
> **Kent:** A very honest-hearted fellow, and as poor as the King.
> **Lear:** If thou be'st as poor for a subject as he's for a king, thou art poor enough. What wouldst thou?
> **Kent:** Service.
> **Lear:** Who wouldst thou serve?
> **Kent:** You.
> **Lear:** Dost thou know me, fellow?
> **Kent:** No, sir; but you have that in your countenance which I would fain call master.
> **Lear:** What's that?
> **Kent:** Authority.
>
> act 1, scene 4, lines 19–30

The ultimate authority in *The Tragedie of King Lear* ought to be the gods but they seem to be uncaring or equivocal. Edmund the Bastard invokes Nature as his goddess, and urges her to stand up for bastards.

What Edmund means by "nature" is antithetical to what Lear regards as the distinction between "natural" and "unnatural." Goneril and Regan in their father's judgment are "unnatural hags." They see their behavior as "natural," as does Edmund.

"Nothing" is a term prevalent in this tragedy. There are thirty-four uses of "nothing" and forty-two of "nature," "natural," "unnatural." The relationship between nothing and nature is a vexed one throughout Shakespeare and is particularly anguished in *The Tragedie of King Lear*. In the Christian argument, God creates nature out of nothingness. The end of nature, according to the Revelation of St. John the Apostle, comes in a return to a restored Eden:

> And he showed me a pure river of water of life, clear as crystal, proceeding out of the throne of God, and of the Lamb.
>
> In the midst of the street of it, and of either side of the river was the tree of life, which bare twelve manner of fruits, and gave fruit every month: and the leaves of the tree *served* to heal the nations with.
>
> Geneva Bible, Revelation 22:1–2

That healing abundance is alien to Lear's tragedy. As the drama closes, Albany, Kent, and Edgar discover that Lear's prophecy has been fulfilled: Nothing has come of nothing. There is no revelation; nature again drifts back to chaos.

Authority, as a concept, is neither Hebrew nor Greek. It is Roman. Hannah Arendt defined authority as an augmentation of the foundations. When Julius Caesar usurped all authority, he did it in the name of returning to the founders of Rome. Though an expedient fiction, all subsequent authority, whether secular or spiritual, is Caesarian and extends that seminal usurpation of power.

No one has worked out the intricate relationship between authority and what we have learned to call "personality." The European Renaissance of Michel Eyquem de Montaigne (1533–1592),

4

Miguel de Cervantes Saavedra (1547–1616), and William Shakespeare (1564–1616) can be said to have inaugurated our sense of personality. Montaigne invents and studies his own personality, Cervantes independently creates the idiosyncratic Don Quixote and the surprisingly witty and sane Sancho Panza, and Shakespeare peoples his heterocosm with myriad people, each with her or his own personality.

Montaigne, skeptical of all prior authority, massively portrays himself with the freedom of a man who begins anew with a tabula rasa of speculation. Cervantes mocks his forerunners and asserts his personal glory that he shares with Don Quixote. Shakespeare, always hidden behind his work, allows the giant personalities of his plays to act and speak for themselves.

Hamlet's knowledge has no limits, because he does not love anyone. Lear's increase in knowledge always augments suffering, because he loves Cordelia and the Fool. Frequently Hamlet plays the part of himself, since he is theatrical to the core. Lear knows nothing of playing; it is alien to his vast nature.

What is authority to Hamlet? You could argue that the dead father assumes that role. Yet Hamlet's relation to the Warrior-King Hamlet seems equivocal. The ghost of King Hamlet expresses no love for his son, but only for Gertrude, now the wife of the usurper and regicide King Claudius. Though Prince Hamlet says, "He was a man, take him for all in all, / I shall not look upon his like again," we wonder about that "all in all." Do we not hear in that the father's lack of love for the son? Yorick, the King's jester, was the child Hamlet's surrogate mother and father, carrying the little boy about on his back: "Here hung those lips that I have kissed I know not how oft." The Prince has no memories of kissing King Hamlet, and cannot we surmise a sorrow at the heart of his mystery?

King Lear has an enormous need to be loved, by his daughter Cordelia in particular. Shakespeare is nothing if not elliptical and we learn to quest for what has been left out. Nothing is said of Queen Lear. Presumably she is deceased, hardly surprising since Lear is well over eighty years of age. Had she survived, there would have been no place for her in the drama. How horrifying it would have been had she shared Lear's privations, exposed out on the heath.

As we first encounter him in the play, Lear is very difficult to love. He wants to abdicate and yet retain all his authority. Incapable of distinguishing between the hypocrisy of Goneril and Regan and the loving recalcitrance of Cordelia, he is given to amazingly fierce misunderstandings, and to furious cursings. And yet from the start we can see that he is venerated by everyone humane and decent in the drama. Kent, Gloucester, Edgar, Albany join Cordelia and the Fool in their love for him, while Goneril, Regan, Cornwall, Oswald loathe him. Edmund the Bastard, the brilliant tactician of evil, neither loves nor hates anyone, and is so alien to Lear that they never exchange a single word anywhere in the play, though they are on stage together for crucial scenes at the start and the finish.

There is something uncanny in Lear's greatness. Shakespeare has combined in the aged King the attributes of fatherhood, monarchy, and divinity.

CHAPTER 2

Meantime We Shall Express Our Darker Purpose

Lear's drama begins with him still offstage. His loyal followers, the Earl of Kent and the Earl of Gloucester, discuss the forthcoming division of the kingdom, which does not alarm them. King James I would not have been amused and the audience probably shared his reaction. Shakespeare introduces the silent and ominous Edmund, bastard son to Gloucester. Insensitively, Gloucester refers to Edmund as the whoreson. The first word spoken by Edmund is "No" and he sounds icily prophetic by assuring Kent: "Sir, I shall study deserving." That ironic understatement reverberates with disasters to come:

> Gloucester: But I have a son, sir, by order of law, some year
> elder than this, who yet is no dearer in my account.
> Though this knave came something saucily to the world
> before he was sent for, yet was his mother fair, there
> was good sport at his making, and the whoreson must
> be acknowledged. Do you know this noble gentleman,
> Edmund?
> Edmund: No, my lord.
> Gloucester: [*to Edmund*] My Lord of Kent. Remember him
> hereafter as my honourable friend.

Edmund: My services to your lordship.

Kent: I must love you, and sue to know you better.

Edmund: [*to Kent*] Sir, I shall study deserving.

act 1, scene 1, lines 18–30

The entrance of the great King is marked by his first speech, baleful and desperately confused:

Meantime we shall express our darker purpose.
Give me the map there. Know that we have divided
In three our kingdom; and 'tis our fast intent
To shake all cares and business from our age,
Conferring them on younger strengths, while we
Unburdened crawl towards death. Our son of Cornwall,
And you, our no less loving son of Albany,
We have this hour a constant will to publish
Our daughters' several dowers, that future strife
May be prevented now.
The two great princes, France and Burgundy,
Great rivals in our youngest daughter's love,
Long in our court have made their amorous sojourn,
And here are to be answered. Tell me, my daughters—
Since now we will divest us both of rule,
Interest of territory, cares of state—
Which of you shall we say doth love us most,
That we our largest bounty may extend
Where nature doth with merit challenge.—Goneril,
Our eldest born, speak first.

act 1, scene 1, lines 35–54

By "darker purpose" Lear may mean his intention to bestow a third of his kingdom upon Cordelia. But "darker" gets away from him. His vision of abdication is unnerving. He will forsake the duties of kingship and "unburdened crawl towards death." Cornwall, Regan's bestial husband, seems to Lear as loving as Albany, the humane spouse of the even more horrible Goneril. Her speech of supposed love for her father breathes hypocrisy:

Sir, I do love you more than word can wield the matter,
Dearer than eyesight, space and liberty,
Beyond what can be valued, rich or rare,
No less than life, with grace, health, beauty, honour.
As much as child e'er loved, or father found,
A love that makes breath poor and speech unable,
Beyond all manner of so much I love you.

act 1, scene 1, lines 55–61

Regan's declaration of daughterly love minces in Goneril's mode and absurdly seeks to surpass it:

Sir I am made of that self mettle as my sister,
And prize me at her worth. In my true heart
I find she names my very deed of love:
Only she comes too short, that I profess
Myself an enemy to all other joys
Which the most precious square of sense possesses,
And find I am alone felicitate
In your dear highness' love.

act 1, scene 1, lines 69–76

In reaction to these monstrous sisters, Cordelia loves and is silent:

Lear: But now our joy,
Although our last and least, to whose young love
The vines of France and milk of Burgundy
Strive to be interested, what can you say to draw
A third more opulent than your sisters? Speak.
Cordelia: Nothing, my lord.
Lear: Nothing?
Cordelia: Nothing.
Lear: Nothing will come of nothing, speak again.
Cordelia: Unhappy that I am, I cannot heave
My heart into my mouth. I love your majesty
According to my bond, no more nor less.
Lear: How, how, Cordelia? Mend your speech a little,
Lest you may mar your fortunes.
Cordelia: Good my lord,
You have begot me, bred me, loved me. I
Return those duties back as are right fit,
Obey you, love you, and most honour you.
Why have my sisters husbands, if they say
They love you all? Hapily when I shall wed,
That lord whose hand must take my plight shall carry
Half my love with him, half my care and duty.
Sure I shall never marry like my sisters
To love my father all.
Lear: But goes thy heart with this?
Cordelia: Ay, my good lord.

Lear: So young and so untender?
Cordelia: So young, my lord, and true.

act 1, scene 1, lines 82–108

"Nothing will come of nothing" to Lear means he will withdraw Cordelia's dowry. He cannot know that he has prophesied the final emptiness that will afflict his world. His furious curse rises suddenly and with amazing violence:

Well, let it be so. Thy truth then be thy dower,
For by the sacred radiance of the sun,
The mysteries of Hecate and the night,
By all the operation of the orbs
From whom we do exist and cease to be,
Here I disclaim all my paternal care,
Propinquity and property of blood,
And as a stranger to my heart and me
Hold thee from this for ever. The barbarous Scythian,
Or he that makes his generation messes
To gorge his appetite, shall to my bosom
Be as well neighboured, pitied and relieved,
As thou my sometime daughter.

act 1, scene 1, lines 109–21

Christopher Marlowe's *Tamburlaine the Great* (1587) established the fashion of viewing the Scythians, who inhabited the Black Sea area, as cruel and barbarous. It can be doubted that they cannibalized their young, but the enraged Lear says that in time of need he would just as soon have aided them as he would his disowned daughter.

11

How can we account for the uncontrolled wrath of a great king previously known for his loving-kindness? What is it in Lear's personality that has opened up to this abyss? Sigmund Freud, in one of his most revealing misreadings, attributed Lear's ferocity to repressed lust for Cordelia. My admiration for Freud as a major essayist, the Montaigne of the twentieth century, is not diminished by his mistaken speculation. Lear desperately needs Cordelia to love him, but not as a sexual partner.

Lear's personality, every inch a king, requires universal reverence and obedience from everyone but particularly Cordelia, since he loves her best. If he is Yahweh, then she is Israel. As the Chosen Person she suffers the fate of Israel.

It hardly matters if one neither trusts nor loves Yahweh. He will not go away. No other literary character approaches his inescapability. James Joyce's Stephen tapped his own forehead and said: "But in here it is I must kill the king and the priest." He would not have said: "But in here it is I must kill God." Nietzsche in *Twilight of the Gods* remarked: "I am afraid we are not rid of God because we still have faith in grammar."

Nietzsche's shrewd insight is based upon Yahweh's pun, when the God orders a reluctant Moses to go down into Egypt to liberate the people of Israel:

But Moses said unto God, Who am I, that I should go unto Pharaoh, and that I should bring the children of Israel out of Egypt?

And he answered, Certainly I will be with thee; and this shall be a token unto thee, that I have sent thee, After that thou hast brought the people out of Egypt, ye shall serve God upon this mountain.

Then Moses said unto God, Behold, *when* I shall come unto the children of Israel, and shall say unto them, The God of your fathers hath sent me unto you; if they say unto me, What is his Name? What shall I say unto them?

And God answered Moses, I AM THAT I AM. Also he said, Thus shalt thou say unto the children of Israel, I AM hath sent me unto you.

Geneva Bible, Exodus 3:11–14

In the Hebrew, Yahweh answers: *ehyeh asher ehyeh*, rendered here as I AM THAT I AM. A closer translation is: I WILL BE [present] I WILL BE. The God will be present wherever and whenever he chooses to be, and therefore absent when and where he so wills. *Ehyeh* puns upon Yahweh. The God is a grim ironist, aware that he is one with all being.

Hamlet plays many variations upon "to be." He seems to know implicitly that divinity and grammar are a unison. Lear has no such knowledge, yet he incarnates the God who identifies all that is with himself. The anger of Yahweh is mirrored in the fury of King Lear, who has no way of understanding when Cordelia bravely asserts her individual being and her wise realization that divided love involves no diminishment.

Lear's insensate vehemence is then turned against Kent, his truest subject:

Kent: Royal Lear,
Whom I have ever honoured as my king,
Loved as my father, as my master followed,
As my great patron thought on in my prayers—
Lear: The bow is bent and drawn; make from the shaft.

13

Kent: Let it fall rather, though the fork invade
The region of my heart: be Kent unmannerly
When Lear is mad. What wouldst thou do, old man?
Think'st thou that duty shall have dread to speak,
When power to flattery bows? To plainness honour's bound
When majesty falls to folly. Reserve thy state,
And in thy best consideration check
This hideous rashness. Answer my life my judgement,
Thy youngest daughter does not love thee least,
Nor are those empty-hearted, whose low sounds
Reverb no hollowness.

act 1, scene 1, lines 140–55

The King proclaims that his bow, once bent and drawn, will send forth the arrow of destruction and that Kent had better avoid the shaft. With great courage, Kent accepts possible execution, and defies courtly decorum by plainly calling his King insanely foolish and an old man falling into nonsense.

Lear: Kent, on thy life, no more.
Kent: My life I never held but as a pawn
To wage against thine enemies, ne'er fear to lose it,
Thy safety being the motive.
Lear: Out of my sight!
Kent: See better, Lear, and let me still remain
The true blank of thine eye.
Lear: Now by Apollo—
Kent: Now by Apollo, King,
Thou swear'st thy gods in vain.

act 1, scene 1, lines 155–62

In a wonderful exchange, Lear shrieks, "Out of my sight!" while Kent urges the King to "see better," a Shakespearean irony proleptic of the long way down and out that Lear and Gloucester must tumble until at last the mad King and blinded Earl learn to see inwardly. It is marvelous that Kent implores to be allowed to remain and continue to be the true blank of Lear's eye. The metaphor of archery culminates in the true blank that is the white spot centering a target. Kent in effect would be the white of Lear's disordered eye. But Kent's wisdom comes close to provoking his King to instant slaughter:

Lear: O vassal! Miscreant!
Albany and Cornwall: Dear sir, forbear!
Kent: Do, kill thy physician, and thy fee bestow
Upon the foul disease. Revoke thy gift,
Or whilst I can vent clamour from my throat
I'll tell thee thou dost evil.
Lear: Hear me, recreant, on thine allegiance, hear me:
That thou hast sought to make us break our vows,
Which we durst never yet, and with strained pride
To come betwixt our sentences and our power,
Which nor our nature, nor our place can bear,
Our potency made good, take thy reward.
Five days we do allot thee for provision,
To shield thee from disasters of the world,
And on the sixth to turn thy hated back
Upon our kingdom. If on the next day following
Thy banished trunk be found in our dominions,
The moment is thy death. Away! By Jupiter,
This shall not be revoked.

act 1, scene 1, lines 162–80

One wishes that this were Lear's nadir, but much worse is to come. A presage is heard in the dialogue between the monstrous sisters, Goneril and Regan:

Goneril: Sister, it is not a little I have to say of what most nearly appertains to us both. I think our father will hence tonight.

Regan: That's most certain, and with you. Next month with us.

Goneril: You see how full of changes his age is. The observation we have made of it hath not been little. He always loved our sister most, and with what poor judgement he hath now cast her off appears too grossly.

Regan: 'Tis the infirmity of his age, yet he hath ever but slenderly known himself.

Goneril: The best and soundest of his time hath been but rash; then must we look from his age to receive not alone the imperfections of long-engraffed condition, but therewithal the unruly waywardness that infirm and choleric years bring with them.

Regan: Such unconstant starts are we like to have from him as this of Kent's banishment.

Goneril: There is further compliment of leave-taking between France and him. Pray you let us hit together. If our father carry authority with such disposition as he bears, this last surrender of his will but offend us.

Regan: We shall further think of it.

Goneril: We must do something, and i' the heat.

act 1, scene 1, lines 285–309

Regan is accurate in saying: "he hath ever but slenderly known himself." Goneril, always more icily intelligent, extends that judgment to everyone in Lear's generation: "The best and soundest of his time hath been but rash." Acutely, she makes an accurate judgment about Lear's nature: "Pray you let us hit together. If our father carry authority with such disposition as he bears, this last surrender of his will but offend us." Hitting together urges agreement on a mutual strike against the father's continued authority. Lear himself, as he abdicated, had insisted, "we shall retain / The name, and all th' addition to a king," where "addition" meant everything that made a king a king. There is no justification for Goneril and Regan, yet Lear has placed himself in an absurd position, king and no king. His darker purpose will prove dark indeed.

CHAPTER 3

Thou, Nature,
Art My Goddess

In Shakespeare, as in life, personality defines itself through juxta-position and contrast with other personalities. Edmund the Bas-tard and Lear represent two extremes that cannot speak to each other. Violent affect marks Lear and, whether it is love or rage, it is always natural, all too natural. What Lear regards as nature is antithetical to Edmund's sense of nature:

Thou, Nature, art my goddess; to thy law
My services are bound. Wherefore should I
Stand in the plague of custom, and permit
The curiosity of nations to deprive me?
For that I am some twelve or fourteen moonshines
Lag of a brother? Why bastard? Wherefore base?
When my dimensions are as well compact,
My mind as generous and my shape as true
As honest madam's issue? Why brand they us
With base? With baseness, bastardy? Base, base?
Who, in the lusty stealth of nature take
More composition and fierce quality
Than doth within a dull stale tired bed

Go to the creating of a whole tribe of fops
Got 'tween a sleep and wake. Well, then,
Legitimate Edgar, I must have your land.
Our father's love is to the bastard Edmund
As to the legitimate. Fine word, 'legitimate'!
Well, my legitimate, if this letter speed
And my invention thrive, Edmund the base
Shall top the legitimate. I grow, I prosper:
Now, gods, stand up for bastards!

                                    act 1, scene 2, lines 1–22

This ironic soliloquy is energized by its rhetorical questions and its obsessive repetitions: "bastard," four times; "legitimate," five times; and "base," six times. There is a mounting crescendo in Edmund's drive to exorcise himself from the stigma of illegitimacy. "Base" in particular grates him.

Faulconbridge, the Bastard in *King John*, is heroic, witty, and admirable in every way. But then he is the natural son of King Richard Lionheart. Don John, in *Much Ado About Nothing*, is called "the Bastard Prince" and is a dismal creature. Edmund defies categorization. In no way does he resemble his father, Gloucester, or his legitimate half brother, Edgar. Shakespeare created Edmund directly after he composed *Othello*, and Iago might seem to provide a paradigm for Edmund. The differences, though, are profound. Iago is a great improviser and weaver of a net around Othello, Desdemona, and Cassio. But Edmund is a genius of the strategy of evil, who improvises only as part of a deep, premeditated design.

Samuel Taylor Coleridge characterized Iago as "motiveless malignancy." I think that Iago's motive is clear enough. He has been passed over by his war god Othello, and seeks vengeance for what Milton's Satan wants to call "a sense of injured merit." What is Edmund's motive? He seeks status through power and is more than willing to betray his father to Cornwall's brutal plucking out of Gloucester's eyeballs. With no animus against Edgar, he reduces his brother to an outcast, who evades execution by assuming the disguise of a Bedlamite beggar. His climactic barbarity is to order the execution of Lear and Cordelia.

Shakespeare must have been aware of the extraordinary disproportion between Edmund's horror of abasement and the crimes against humanity to which it leads. What would have happened if Edmund's design had been fulfilled? Goneril, after poisoning Regan, presumably would have joined with Edmund in murdering Albany. Since Edmund lacks almost all affect, he would have disposed of Goneril soon enough. But what would he have possessed had he become King?

If there is an answer to these questions, the aptest prelude can be found in Edmund's final soliloquy in the drama:

To both these sisters have I sworn my love,
Each jealous of the other, as the stung
Are of the adder. Which of them shall I take?
Both? One? Or neither? Neither can be enjoyed
If both remain alive. To take the widow
Exasperates, makes mad her sister Goneril,
And hardly shall I carry out my side,
Her husband being alive. Now then, we'll use
His countenance for the battle, which being done,
Let her who would be rid of him devise
His speedy taking off. As for the mercy
Which he intends to Lear and to Cordelia,

The battle done, and they within our power,
Shall never see his pardon; for my state
Stands on me to defend, not to debate.

act 5, scene 1, lines 56–70

With characteristic coolness, Edmund surveys his tangled situation. He has made love both to Goneril and Regan and promised each a permanent union. One can delight in the insouciance with which this fusion of a Machiavel and Don Juan contemplates a double date with two monsters of the deep. Albany's authority will be exploited for the battle against Cordelia and the French, after which Goneril can be relied upon to extinguish him. Lear and Cordelia will be executed, and the state will be Edmund's, a solitary survivor.

Despite his brilliance and his total obsession with baseness, Edmund has no realization that he has destroyed himself. He does not know that Edgar, defending their blind father, has slain the vicious Oswald, and found on the corpse Goneril's letter to Edmund, in which she urges the slaughter of Albany. The painful transformation of the gullible Edgar will complete itself when, at the cry of the trumpet, a masked and nameless knight attired in black enters to strike down his bastard half brother. The wheel comes full circle. Edmund has created a new Edgar, against whom he has no chance of victory. He has become one of Shakespeare's "fools of time":

If my dear love were but the child of state
It might, for fortune's bastard, be unfathered,
As subject to time's love or to time's hate,
Weeds among weeds, or flowers with flowers gathered.

No, it was builded far from accident;
It suffers not in smiling pomp, nor falls
Under the blow of thralled discontent,
Whereto th'inviting time our fashion calls:
It fears not policy, that heretic,
Which works on leases of short-numbered hours,
But all alone stands hugely politic,
That it nor grows with heat, nor drowns with showers.
    To this I witness call the fools of time,
    Which die for goodness, who have lived for crime.

                                        Sonnet 124

Edmund, fortune's bastard, has lived for crime. We will yet see him die, if not for goodness, then desperately, in a vain attempt to change his nature.

CHAPTER 4

Now Thou Art an O
Without a Figure

The first mention of Lear's Fool comes when the King notices his absence. A knight remarks that since Cordelia has been exiled to France, the Fool has pined away. Entering, he immediately displays bitterness at her fate, and taunts Lear with adages and a weird chant:

Fool: Mark it, nuncle:
>Have more than thou showest,
>Speak less than thou knowest,
>Lend less than thou owest,
>Ride more than thou goest,
>Learn more than thou trowest,
>Set less than thou throwest,
>Leave thy drink and thy whore
>And keep in-a-door,
>And thou shalt have more
>Than two tens to a score.

Kent: This is nothing, fool.
Fool: Then 'tis like the breath of an unfee'd lawyer, you gave

me nothing for't. [*to Lear*] Can you make no use of
nothing, nuncle?

Lear: Why, no, boy; nothing can be made out of nothing.

act 1, scene 4, lines 115–30

Lear repeats his dialogue with Cordelia:

Cordelia: Nothing, my lord.
Lear: Nothing?
Cordelia: Nothing.
Lear: Nothing will come of nothing, speak again.

act 1, scene 1, lines 87–90

Is Lear on some level cognizant that he is obsessed with "nothing"? Remorselessly the Fool presses on:

Lear: Dost thou call me fool, boy?
Fool: All thy other titles thou hast given away; that thou wast
born with.
Kent: This is not altogether fool, my lord.
Fool: No, faith, lords and great men will not let me; if I had a
monopoly out, they would have part on't; and ladies too,
they will not let me have all the fool to myself, they'll be
snatching. Nuncle, give me an egg and I'll give thee two
crowns.
Lear: What two crowns shall they be?
Fool: Why, after I have cut the egg i'the middle and eat up
the meat, the two crowns of the egg. When thou clovest
thy crown i'the middle and gav'st away both parts, thou
bor'st thine ass on thy back o'er the dirt. Thou hadst little

wit in thy bald crown when thou gav'st thy golden one
away. If I speak like myself in this, let him be whipped
that first finds it so.

[*Sings.*] Fools had ne'er less grace in a year,
　　　For wise men are grown foppish,
　　　And know not how their wits to wear,
　　　Their manners are so apish.

act 1, scene 4, lines 141–61

Lear knows and does not know what his beloved Fool intends
to mean. His pained awareness that his abdication was a mishap is
egged on by the Fool's dark wit:

Lear: When were you wont to be so full of songs, sirrah?
Fool: I have used it, nuncle, e'er since thou mad'st thy
　　　daughters thy mothers; for when thou gav'st them the
　　　rod, and putt'st down thine own breeches,
　　　[*Sings.*] Then they for sudden joy did weep
　　　　　And I for sorrow sung,
　　　　　That such a king should play bo-peep,
　　　　　And go the fools among.
　　　Prithee, nuncle, keep a schoolmaster that can teach thy
　　　fool to lie; I would fain learn to lie.
Lear: And you lie, sirrah, we'll have you whipped.
Fool: I marvel what kin thou and thy daughters are. They'll
　　　have me whipped for speaking true, thou'lt have me
　　　whipped for lying, and sometimes I am whipped for
　　　holding my peace. I had rather be any kind o'thing than
　　　a fool, and yet I would not be thee, nuncle. Thou hast
　　　pared thy wit o'both sides, and left nothing i'the middle.

27

Here comes one o'the parings.
Enter Goneril.

act 1, scene 4, lines 162–79

Wit, wildly varied throughout Shakespeare, here is plain common sense. Poor Lear has rendered himself devoid of that crucial quality and is now at the mercy of Goneril and Regan. The Fool is quick to emphasize the great King's helplessness:

Lear: How now, daughter? What makes that frontlet on?
   Methinks you are too much of late i'the frown.
Fool: Thou wast a pretty fellow when thou hadst no need to care
   for her frowning. Now thou art an O without a figure; I
   am better than thou art now. I am a fool, thou art nothing.
   [*to Goneril*] Yes, forsooth, I will hold my tongue; so your
   face bids me, though you say nothing. Mum, mum!
      He that keeps nor crust nor crumb,
      Weary of all, shall want some.
[*Points to Lear.*] That's a shelled peascod.

act 1, scene 4, lines 180–90

With cruel accuracy, the Fool characterizes Lear as zero, without any preceding numeral. The King is not even a Fool; he is nothing. But what kind of being is Lear's Fool? There is something uncanny about him. Is he old or young? We do not know. Is he a changeling, one of the faery folk? Can he die? He simply vanishes from the play, and Lear confounds him with the lost Cordelia:

And my poor fool is hanged! No, no, no life!

act 5, scene 3, line 304

In Shakespeare, there are several meanings of "fool." It can mean a dear one, or a child, or a jester, or a victim, as it does throughout the tragedies. Lear's Fool is unique in the searing quality of his bitter wit, and his unrelenting assault upon the King's folly. It is not too much to say that the Fool hastens the onset of Lear's madness and prolongs its intensity.

When the Fool points to Lear and says "That's a shelled peascod," the cruel implication is that the King has become nothing, a pod emptied out, castrated. Defied by Goneril, Lear breaks forth in a lament for his lost identity:

> Lear: Does any here know me? Why, this is not Lear. Does
>   Lear walk thus, speak thus? Where are his eyes? Either
>   his notion weakens, or his discernings are lethargied—
>   Ha! sleeping or waking? Sure 'tis not so. Who is it that
>   can tell me who I am?
> Fool: Lear's shadow.
> Lear: I would learn that, for by the marks of sovereignty,
>   knowledge and reason, I should be false persuaded I had
>   daughters.
> Fool: Which they will make an obedient father.
> Lear: Your name, fair gentlewoman?
>
> act 1, scene 4, lines 217–27

The Fool's blunt eloquence—"Lear's shadow"—could not be bettered. He is Lear's shadow, indicating the King's transformation into a fool, and the transmutation of royal substance into nothing.

CHAPTER 5

O Let Me Not Be Mad, Not Mad, Sweet Heaven!

The celerity of Lear's fury marks again his descent from the Bible's Yahweh. When Goneril dismisses half his retinue of knights, he calls up darkness and devils, and names her a degenerate bastard:

Lear: Detested kite, thou liest.
My train are men of choice and rarest parts
That all particulars of duty know,
And in the most exact regard support
The worships of their name. O most small fault,
How ugly didst thou in Cordelia show,
Which like an engine wrenched my frame of nature
From the fixed place, drew from my heart all love
And added to the gall. O Lear, Lear, Lear!
[*striking his head*] Beat at this gate, that let thy folly in
And thy dear judgement out. Go, go, my people.

                                        act 1, scene 4, lines 254–64

Lear names her accurately as an abomination, a cruel hawk, and realizes belatedly his error concerning Cordelia. He strikes his own head to punish it for thrusting judgment out and letting folly in. Shakespeare ironically echoes Edmund's soliloquy in Lear's curse of Goneril:

> **Lear:** Hear, Nature, hear, dear goddess, hear:
> Suspend thy purpose, if thou didst intend
> To make this creature fruitful.
> Into her womb convey sterility,
> Dry up in her the organs of increase,
> And from her derogate body never spring
> A babe to honour her. If she must teem,
> Create her child of spleen, that it may live
> And be a thwart disnatured torment to her.
> Let it stamp wrinkles in her brow of youth,
> With cadent tears fret channels in her cheeks,
> Turn all her mother's pains and benefits
> To laughter and contempt, that she may feel
> How sharper than a serpent's tooth it is
> To have a thankless child. Away, away!
>
> act 1, scene 4, lines 269–81

Edmund appealed to Nature in a very different sense and implored her to stand up for bastards. Lear distorts a creative Nature and urges a disnaturing by which Goneril's putative daughter will be a torment to her. He has begun the process by which his own worship of Nature, as benign lord, gives way to a sense of malevolence. Lear falls away into an abyss where monsters of the deep—Goneril, Regan, Cornwall—prey upon everyone until, at last, they prey upon themselves.

What Lear finally will discover is the abyss within himself. Shakespeare, who invented a new kind of man in Hamlet, now unearths a very old mode of the human, one in which you gaze out at an abyss, and then are shocked into realizing that you behold a mirror image of yourself. Lear's greatness, whatever it was in the past, is in abeyance until he begins to wander on the heath, exposed to all the injustice of the skies.

Departing for Regan's court, Lear and the Fool commence a further stage in what will be the great King's madness:

> Fool: The reason why the seven stars are no more than seven is
> a pretty reason.
> Lear: Because they are not eight.
> Fool: Yes, indeed, thou wouldst make a good fool.
> Lear: To take't again perforce—monster ingratitude!
> Fool: If thou wert my fool, nuncle, I'd have thee beaten for
> being old before thy time.
> Lear: How's that?
> Fool: Thou shouldst not have been old till thou hadst been wise.
> Lear: O let me not be mad, not mad, sweet heaven! I would
> not be mad.
> Keep me in temper, I would not be mad.
>
> act 1, scene 5, lines 33–44

Does this mark the onset of Lear's madness? I think not. Yet a change has begun and will devastate him. Soon enough we hear the cadence of ominous calamity:

> O, how this mother swells up toward my heart!
> *Hysterica passio*, down, thou climbing sorrow,
> Thy element's below.
>
> act 2, scene 2, lines 246–48

"Hysterica Passio," called in the English vernacular "the mother," afflicted both men and women. It caused a painful swelling, and was attributed to the womb, even in a male. I hardly believe that Lear finds the origin of his madness in what certain brilliant feminists call an asphyxiating maternal womb. He will learn that his own fury is his illness.

CHAPTER 6

Poor Tom! /
That's Something Yet:
Edgar I Nothing Am

It is infrequently realized that, after Lear himself, the crucial personality in the drama is Edgar, legitimate son of Gloucester, and godson of Lear. Lear speaks 749 lines, Edgar 392, which is more than anyone else. Surprisingly Kent speaks 368, while Gloucester speaks 338, and I think we neglect Kent's role. Edmund at 307 lines is the counterpoise to Edgar, and I will argue that, for all his malevolent triumph, he is less of a challenge to our imagination than is Edgar.

I am startled that the Fool has only 227 lines, since they are so memorable. It might be expected that the descending order after that would be Goneril at 199, Regan at 190, and the perplexed Albany at 159. Poor Cordelia, absent in her exile and then martyred in her return, speaks only 117 lines, just 8 more than the bestial Cornwall. At 78 lines, the wretched Oswald completes the principal speaking roles.

Both quartos (1608, 1619) of *King Lear* give prominence to Edgar on their title pages:

True Chronicle Historie of the life and
death of King LEAR and his three
Daughters.
With the vnfortunate life of Edgar, *sonne*
and heire to the Earle of Gloster, and his
sullen and assumed humor of
TOM of Bedlam

"Sullen" might derive from the Anglo-French *solain*, and so
would be related to the Latin *solus* ("alone"). In Canto VII of the
Inferno, Dante shows those who were sullen in the sweet air, and
now must speak through mud up to their mouth. This was once
called *acedia*, "the malady of monks."

Edgar's "humor" stems from the ancient belief that each of
us contained four fluids—blood, phlegm, black bile, and yellow
bile—and that the balance between the fluids determined our
temperament and health. By the later 1500s, humor simply meant
temperament. Edgar's personality, traumatized by Edmund's
betrayal, indeed becomes both sullen and assumed.

Edmund's subtle weaving traps both Gloucester and Edgar.
Though benign, Gloucester has little intelligence, while Edgar
begins as a trusting youth. Shakespeare grants Edmund astonishing deftness at writing with the lives of his father and brother, even
as Iago weaves his net with Othello, Cassio, and Desdemona.

Gloucester: Kent banished thus? and France in choler parted?
And the King gone tonight? Prescribed his power,
Confined to exhibition? All this done
Upon the gad?—Edmund, how now, what news?
Edmund: [*Pockets the letter.*] So please your lordship, none.

Gloucester: Why so earnestly seek you to put up that letter?

Edmund: I know no news, my lord.

Gloucester: What paper were you reading?

Edmund: Nothing, my lord.

Gloucester: No? What needed then that terrible dispatch of it into your pocket? The quality of nothing hath not such need to hide itself. Let's see.—Come, if it be nothing, I shall not need spectacles.

act 1, scene 2, lines 23–36

"Nothing" brings us back to Lear and the Fool, and the tolling bell of "nothing" resonates throughout the drama.

Edmund: I beseech you, sir, pardon me. It is a letter from my brother that I have not all o'er-read; and for so much as I have perused, I find it not fit for your o'er-looking.

Gloucester: Give me the letter, sir.

Edmund: I shall offend, either to detain or give it. The contents, as in part I understand them, are to blame.

Gloucester: Let's see, let's see.

Edmund: I hope, for my brother's justification, he wrote this but as an essay, or taste of my virtue.

Gloucester: [*Reads.*] 'This policy, and reverence of age, makes the world bitter to the best of our times, keeps our fortunes from us till our oldness cannot relish them. I begin to find an idle and fond bondage in the oppression of aged tyranny, who sways not as it hath power, but as it is suffered. Come to me, that of this I may speak more. If our father would sleep till I waked him, you should enjoy half his revenue for ever and live the beloved of your brother. Edgar.' Hum! Conspiracy! 'Sleep till I wake him, you should enjoy half his revenue.'—My son Edgar, had he a hand to write this? A heart and brain to breed it in? When came this to you? Who brought it?

Edmund: It was not brought me, my lord, there's the cunning of it. I found it thrown in at the casement of my closet.

Gloucester: You know the character to be your brother's?

Edmund: If the matter were good, my lord, I durst swear it were his; but in respect of that, I would fain think it were not.

Gloucester: It is his?

Edmund: It is his hand, my lord; but I hope his heart is not in the contents.

Gloucester: Has he never before sounded you in this business?

Edmund: Never, my lord. But I have heard him oft maintain it to be fit that, sons at perfect age and fathers declined, the father should be as ward to the son and the son manage his revenue.

Gloucester: O villain, villain! His very opinion in the letter. Abhorred villain! Unnatural, detested, brutish villain— worse than brutish! Go, sirrah, seek him. I'll apprehend him. Abominable villain! Where is he?

act 1, scene 2, lines 37–78

One wonders that Gloucester is so quick to believe Edmund. Generational strife pervades *King Lear*. Even so, something in Gloucester seems undone by the King's self-destructive quasi-abdication. He sends Edmund to bring back Edgar, and Shakespeare juxtaposes Gloucester's confused musings with Edmund's cold delight in response:

Gloucester: These late eclipses in the sun and moon portend
no good to us. Though the wisdom of Nature can reason
it thus and thus, yet nature finds itself scourged by the
sequent effects. Love cools, friendship falls off, brothers
divide: in cities, mutinies; in countries, discord; in palaces,
treason; and the bond cracked 'twixt son and father. This
villain of mine comes under the prediction—there's
son against father. The King falls from bias of nature—
there's father against child. We have seen the best of
our time. Machinations, hollowness, treachery, and all
ruinous disorders follow us disquietly to our graves.
Find out this villain, Edmund; it shall lose thee nothing.
Do it carefully.—And the noble and true-hearted Kent
banished, his offence honesty! 'Tis strange, strange!

Exit.

Edmund: This is the excellent foppery of the world, that when
we are sick in fortune, often the surfeits of our own
behaviour, we make guilty of our disasters the sun, the
moon and the stars, as if we were villains on necessity, fools
by heavenly compulsion, knaves, thieves, and treachers by
spherical predominance; drunkards, liars and adulterers
by an enforced obedience of planetary influence; and all
that we are evil in by a divine thrusting on. An admirable
evasion of whoremaster man, to lay his goatish disposition
on the charge of a star. My father compounded with my
mother under the dragon's tail and my nativity was under
Ursa Major, so that it follows I am rough and lecherous.
Fut! I should have been that I am had the maidenliest
star in the firmament twinkled on my bastardizing.

act 1, scene 2, lines 103–33

Gloucester speaks for the audience's concern in 1605 about succession, two years after the death of Elizabeth and the advent of James I. "Nature" is heard three times, inexorably followed by "it shall lose thee nothing." "We have seen the best of our time" portends this most tragic of tragedies. Overcome by strangeness, Gloucester commences his movement from figurative to literal blindness.

Edmund brims with negative exuberance in his mordant soliloquy, after his father's departure. Dismissing all stupidity, including astrological nonsense, he affirms his disposition with alacrity, and returns to his status as bastard. With Edgar's entrance, Edmund again contrives his own comedy, casting his brother as victim:

Edmund: Pat he comes, like the catastrophe of the old
  comedy. My cue is villainous melancholy, with a sigh
  like Tom o'Bedlam.—O, these eclipses do portend these
  divisions. Fa, sol, la, mi.

Edgar: How now, brother Edmund, what serious
  contemplation are you in?

Edmund: I am thinking, brother, of a prediction I read this
  other day, what should follow these eclipses.

Edgar: Do you busy yourself with that?

Edmund: I promise you, the effects he writes of succeed
  unhappily, as of unnaturalness between the child and
  the parent, death, dearth, dissolutions of ancient amities,
  divisions in state, menaces and maledictions against King
  and nobles, needless diffidences, banishment of friends,
  dissipation of cohorts, nuptial breaches and I know not
  what.

Edgar: How long have you been a sectary astronomical?

Edmund: Come, come, when saw you my father last?

Edgar: Why, the night gone by.

Edmund: Spake you with him?

Edgar: Ay, two hours together.

Edmund: Parted you in good terms? Found you no displeasure in him, by word nor countenance?

Edgar: None at all.

Edmund: Bethink yourself wherein you may have offended him, and at my entreaty forbear his presence till some little time hath qualified the heat of his displeasure; which at this instant so rageth in him, that with the mischief of your person it would scarcely allay.

Edgar: Some villain hath done me wrong.

Edmund: That's my fear. I pray you, have a continent forbearance till the speed of his rage goes slower; and, as I say, retire with me to my lodging, from whence I will fitly bring you to hear my lord speak. Pray ye, go: there's my key. If you do stir abroad, go armed.

Edgar: Armed, brother!

Edmund: Brother, I advise you to the best, go armed. I am no honest man if there be any good meaning towards you. I have told you what I have seen and heard—but faintly; nothing like the image and horror of it. Pray you, away!

Edgar: Shall I hear from you anon?

Edmund: I do serve you in this business.

                              act 1, scene 2, lines 134–76

We are grimly charmed by Edmund's theatricalism. He makes Edgar into the catastrophe or culmination of an antique comedy, while taking his own cue as the assumed melancholy of the villain. Uncannily he prophesies what he cannot know, Edgar's assumption of the disguise of Tom o' Bedlam. Mocking Gloucester's language, he sings out a "Fa, sol, la, mi," a discordant variation on the fourth, fifth, sixth, and third notes of the C major scale.

A different tonality is invoked, as Edmund surpasses his father in previewing the consequences of unnaturalness. The difference is that Edmund himself will be the chief cause of overturn in the family, the kingdom, and at last in the world:

Edmund: A credulous father and a brother noble,
Whose nature is so far from doing harms
That he suspects none—on whose foolish honesty
My practices ride easy. I see the business.
Let me, if not by birth, have lands by wit;
All with me's meet that I can fashion fit.

act 1, scene 2, lines 177–82

As always, Edmund is precise and accurate. Gloucester and Edgar are by nature incapable of apprehending evil. What Edmund calls wit is Machiavellian cunning. He cannot know, however, that he has created a new Edgar, who will forge a painful identity as an inexorable avenger.

In transition, Edgar is given a crucial soliloquy:

I heard myself proclaimed,
And by the happy hollow of a tree
Escaped the hunt. No port is free, no place
That guard and most unusual vigilance
Does not attend my taking. While I may scape

I will preserve myself, and am bethought
To take the basest and most poorest shape
That ever penury in contempt of man
Brought near to beast. My face I'll grime with filth,
Blanket my loins, elf all my hairs in knots,
And with presented nakedness outface
The winds and persecutions of the sky.
The country gives me proof and precedent
Of Bedlam beggars, who, with roaring voices,
Strike in their numbed and mortified bare arms
Pins, wooden pricks, nails, sprigs of rosemary;
And with this horrible object, from low farms,
Poor pelting villages, sheepcotes and mills,
Sometime with lunatic bans, sometime with prayers,
Enforce their charity. Poor Turlygod, poor Tom!
That's something yet: Edgar I nothing am.

                              act 2, scene 2, lines 172–92

Now an outlaw, Edgar begins to draw upon his hidden resources. Needing a disguise, he descends to the absolute bottom of the social scale. He becomes Poor Tom o' Bedlam, a homeless vagrant and beggar no longer confined to the madhouse of Bethlehem Hospital. In a manuscript commonplace book of 1620 or so, there is an astonishing poem marked by Shakespeare's influence. To me it has always seemed the greatest anonymous poem in the English language, a "Tom o' Bedlam's Song" worthy of the poet of *King Lear*:

From the hag and hungry goblin
    That into rags would rend ye,

The spirit that stands by the naked man
    In the Book of Moons defend ye,
That of your five sound senses
    You never be forsaken
Nor wander from yourselves, with Tom,
    Abroad to beg your bacon.
While I do sing, "Any food, any feeding
    Feeding, drink, or clothing?"
Come dame or maid, be not afraid:
    Poor Tom will injure nothing . . .

When I short have shorn my sow's-face
    And swigged my horny barrel,
At an oaken inn I impound my skin
    In a suit of gilt apparel.
The Moon's my constant mistress
    And the lovely owl my marrow,
The flaming drake and the night-crow make
    Me music to my sorrow.
While I do sing "Any food, any feeding
    Feeding, drink or clothing?"
Come dame or maid, be not afraid:
    Poor Tom will injure nothing.

There are several versions of this lyric, but this is the strongest.
A visionary intensity of Shakespearean eloquence breaks through
the rough rhetoric to the uncanny Romanticism of:

The Moon's my constant mistress
    And the lovely owl my marrow,

The flaming drake and the night-crow make
    Me music to my sorrow.

From this midpoint the poem mounts higher:

The palsy plagues my pulses
    When I prig your pigs or pullen,
Your culvers take, or matchless make
    Your Chanticlere or Solan!
When I want provant, with Humphrey
    I sup, and when benighted
I repose in Paul's with waking souls
    Yet never am affrighted.
But I do sing "Any food, any feeding
    Feeding, drink or clothing?"
Come dame or maid, be not afraid:
    Poor Tom will injure nothing.

I know more than Apollo,
    For oft when he lies sleeping
I see the stars at bloody wars
    In the wounded welkin weeping,
The moon embrace her shepherd
    And the Queen of Love her warrior,
While the first doth horn the Star of Morn
    And the next, the Heavenly Farrier.
While I do sing "Any food, any feeding
    Feeding, drink or clothing?"
Come dame or maid, be not afraid:
    Poor Tom will injure nothing.

This is premonitory of Shelley in its exaltation of poetic imagination over classical wisdom. The high lyricism goes on to an Ariel-like delicacy:

The gypsies, Snap and Pedro
    Are none of Tom's comradoes;
The punk I scorn and the cut-purse sworn,
    And the roaring-boy's bravadoes.
The meek, the white, the gentle
    Me handle, touch and spare not,
But those that cross Tom Rhinosceros
    Do what the Panther dare not.
Although I do sing "Any food, any feeding
    Feeding, drink or clothing?"
Come dame or maid, be not afraid:
    Poor Tom will injure nothing.

I hear a Shakespearean touch again in:

The meek, the white, the gentle
    Me handle, touch and spare not,
But those that cross Tom Rhinosceros
    Do what the Panther dare not.

Wonderful as the poem is to this point, its final stanza is a triumph of imaginative vision:

With an host of furious fancies
    Whereof I am commander,
With a burning spear, and a horse of air

To the wilderness I wander.
By a knight of ghosts and shadows
    I summoned am to Tourney
Ten leagues beyond the wide world's end—
    Methinks it is no journey.
Yet I do sing "Any food, any feeding
    Feeding, drink or clothing?"
Come dame or maid, be not afraid:
    Poor Tom will injure nothing.

Why bring this Mad Song to the apprehension of Edgar? "Poor Tom! / That's something yet: Edgar I nothing am." Edgar has chosen to be the naked thing itself, the human reduced by abnegation to negate "I am." Nothing has come to nothing yet Edgar will prove to be as strong as he is subtle. There is an element of self-punishment in his disguise. He could have chosen Kent's path and reappeared as Lear's servant. Shakespeare wants the wheel to come full circle. Edgar will rise from humiliation to a suffering hero, and his metamorphosis will be one of Shakespeare's most powerful and enigmatic inventions.

CHAPTER 7

O Heavens! /
if Yourselves Are Old, /
Make It Your Cause

Fleeing to Regan, the furious Lear discovers that she and Goneril are in league against him. When Goneril enters to join her sister, the King implores the skies for aid:

> O heavens!
> If you do love old men, if your sweet sway
> Allow obedience, if you yourselves are old,
> Make it your cause. Send down, and take my part!
>
> act 2, scene 2, lines 378–81

Charles Lamb, the great Romantic essayist, thought *King Lear* to be unactable, and cited this passage. I myself have never seen an actor who could handle this moment. Sometimes I think that *King Lear* has become less and less actable as the hungry generations tread one another down. If there is no awe to fatherhood, kingship, divinity, then the glory has departed.

Regan urges her father to accept his weakness, but that is intolerable for him. When the dreadful sisters suggest he does not need even a single knight, the King's ineffectual wrath ignites:

> O, reason not the need! Our basest beggars
> Are in the poorest thing superfluous;
> Allow not nature more than nature needs,
> Man's life is cheap as beast's. Thou art a lady;
> If only to go warm were gorgeous,
> Why, nature needs not what though gorgeous wear'st,
> Which scarcely keeps thee warm. But for true need—
> You heavens, give me that patience, patience I need!
> You see me here, you gods, a poor old man,
> As full of grief as age, wretched in both:
> If it be you that stirs these daughters' hearts
> Against their father, fool me not so much
> To bear it tamely; touch me with noble anger,
> And let not women's weapons, water-drops,
> Stain my man's cheeks. No, you unnatural hags,
> I will have such revenges on you both
> That all the world shall—I will do such things—
> What they are yet I know not, but they shall be
> The terrors of the earth! You think I'll weep,
> No, I'll not weep.   *Storm and tempest.*
> I have full cause of weeping, but this heart
> Shall break into a hundred thousand flaws
> Or e'er I'll weep. O fool, I shall go mad.
>
> act 2, scene 2, lines 453–75

Uncannily Lear gives us a prolepsis of Edgar's disguise as a Bedlamite beggar, and the triple use of "nature" is set off by the perfectly apt "unnatural hags." Lear's disdain for tears is more royal than male. Great kings do not weep. But Lear approaches a limit bordering upon madness. It is pitiful to hear him vowing vengeance beyond his power and unknown to him. Shakespeare, superb at timing, punctuates these hapless protestations with the sudden onset of storm and tempest. Lear indeed will die of heartbreak, which excuses the hyperbolical "hundred thousand flaws" or windblown fragments. The great outcry "O fool, I shall go mad" heralds the waning of the great King's glory and his might.

The disguised Kent encounters a knight who describes Lear's agon with the storm:

Contending with the fretful elements;
Bids the wind blow the earth into the sea,
Or swell the curled waters 'bove the main,
That things might change, or cease; tears his white hair,
Which the impetuous blasts with eyeless rage
Catch in their fury and make nothing of,
Strives in his little world of man to outscorn
The to and fro conflicting wind and rain;
This night wherein the cub-drawn bear would couch,
The lion and the belly-pinched wolf
Keep their fur dry, unbonneted he runs,
And bids what will take all.

act 3, scene 1, lines 4–15

Exposed to the elements Lear runs on, scorning the wild wind and rain, and crying out that the universe can disintegrate, for all he cares:

Blow winds and crack your cheeks! Rage, blow!
Your cataracts and hurricanoes, spout
Till you have drenched our steeples, drowned the cocks!
You sulphurous and thought-executing fires,
Vaunt-couriers of oak-cleaving thunderbolts,
Singe my white head! And thou, all-shaking thunder,
Strike flat the thick rotundity o'the world,
Crack nature's moulds, all germens spill at once
That make ingrateful man!

act 3, scene 2, lines 1–9

Shakespeare heaps up images of cosmic destruction. Steeples and weathercocks are to be deluged. Lightning bolts become thought-executing fires. Lear is not calling for the destruction of thought but of his outraged sense of ingratitude. Thunderbolts accompany these precursors. The oak sacred to Jupiter is to be divided, even as Lear split up his kingdom. All the earth is to be flattened, or aborted, and all natural forms are to crack apart, their seeds or germens spilled like semen, so as to end the birth of more ingrates.

The desperate Fool urges Lear to yield to his monster daughters, but that provokes the anguished King to delirium that mingles defiance and self-pity:

Rumble thy bellyful! Spit fire, spout rain!
Nor rain, wind, thunder, fire are my daughters;
I tax not you, you elements, with unkindness.
I never gave you kingdom, called you children;
You owe me no subscription. Why then, let fall
Your horrible pleasure. Here I stand your slave,

A poor, infirm, weak and despised old man.
But yet I call you servile ministers
That will with two pernicious daughters join
Your high-engendered battles 'gainst a head
So old and white as this. O ho! 'tis foul.

act 3, scene 2, lines 14–24

There is magnificent pride in Lear's acceptance of slavery to the heavens, and in his Promethean scorn of their servile ministry. He stands up against the gods, and achieves a bitter heroism.

Under the pelting of the storm, Lear struggles desperately to regain his royal dignity:

No, I will be the pattern of all patience,
I will say nothing.

act 3, scene 2, lines 38–39

The King is hardly patient Job, who actually was scarcely patient. Yet there is deep pathos when he adds: "I will say nothing."

"Nothing," the dark refrain and ultimate conclusion of his tragedy, can be said. Shakespeare's art is to show the myriad nuances of "nothing." When the disguised Kent enters to lead Lear and the Fool to a hovel, he warns that:

Man's nature cannot carry
Th'affliction, nor the fear.

act 3, scene 2, lines 48–49

The great King's response shatters:

> Let the great gods
> That keep this dreadful pudder o'er our heads
> Find out their enemies now. Tremble, thou wretch,
> That hast within thee undivulged crimes,
> Unwhipped of justice. Hide thee, thou bloody hand,
> Thou perjured, and thou simular of virtue
> That art incestuous.

"Pudder" is an uproar; "simular" is a sham chastity. Hidden guilts urge to break forth and "rive" (rend apart) their continental boundaries:

> Caitiff, to pieces shake,
> That under covert and convenient seeming
> Hast practised on man's life. Close pent-up guilts
> Rive your concealing continents and cry
> These dreadful summoners grace. I am a man
> More sinned against than sinning.
>
> act 3, scene 2, lines 49–60

They must cry or beg mercy from the gods' fearful summoners, who order all of us to judgment. Most memorable is Lear's poignant plea:

> I am a man
> More sinned against than sinning.

Though this is incontrovertible, it comforts not at all. Yet who would not be touched when Lear turns from his own suffering to sympathy for his Fool:

My wits begin to turn.
[*to the Fool*] Come on, my boy. How dost my boy? Art cold?
I am cold myself. [*to Kent*] Where is this straw, my fellow?
The art of our necessities is strange,
That can make vile things precious. Come; your hovel.
[*to the Fool*] Poor fool and knave, I have one part in my heart
That's sorry yet for thee.

act 3, scene 2, lines 67–73

Shakespeare, as always, is his own best interpreter. I could not better characterize both the tragedy and Lear himself than as "the art of our necessities is strange."

CHAPTER 8

This Cold Night
Will Turn Us All
to Fools and Madmen

That art, rich and strange, increases its magnitude as Lear continues to defy the stormy heavens:

> Kent: Here is the place, my lord: good my lord, enter;
> The tyranny of the open night's too rough
> For nature to endure.
> *Storm still.*
> Lear: Let me alone.
> Kent: Good my lord, enter here.
> Lear: Wilt break my heart?
> Kent: I had rather break mine own. Good my lord, enter.
> Lear: Thou think'st 'tis much that this contentious storm
> Invades us to the skin: so 'tis to thee,
> But where the greater malady is fixed,
> The lesser is scarce felt. Thou'dst shun a bear,
> But if thy flight lay toward the roaring sea,
> Thou'dst meet the bear i'the mouth. When the mind's free,
> The body's delicate: this tempest in my mind

Doth from my senses take all feeling else,
Save what beats there, filial ingratitude.
Is it not as this mouth should tear this hand
For lifting food to't? But I will punish home;
No, I will weep no more. In such a night
To shut me out? Pour on, I will endure.
In such a night as this? O Regan, Goneril,
Your old, kind father, whose frank heart gave you all—
O, that way madness lies, let me shun that;
No more of that.

Kent: Good my lord, enter here.

Lear: Prithee go in thyself, seek thine own ease.
This tempest will not give me leave to ponder
On things would hurt me more. But I'll go in;
[*to the Fool*] In boy, go first. You houseless poverty—
Nay, get thee in. I'll pray, and then I'll sleep. [*Exit Fool.*]
[*Kneels.*] Poor naked wretches, wheresoe'er you are,
That bide the pelting of this pitiless storm,
How shall your houseless heads and unfed sides,
Your looped and windowed raggedness, defend you
From seasons such as these? O, I have ta'en
Too little care of this. Take physic, pomp,
Expose thyself to feel what wretches feel,
That thou mayst shake the superflux to them
And show the heavens more just.

                                    act 3, scene 4, lines 1–36

Lear opposes his inner tempest to the outward pounding, but vicissitudes have reduced him to a medley of confusions. Nevertheless he recovers his universe of feeling, and for the first time extends it, when he kneels and prays for others unknown to him. I do not think he is acquiring a social conscience, which would be alien to his majesty. Instead he seeks to purge himself of the blindness of pomp, and expose his ruined authority to the pelting his poorest subjects undergo. "Superflux," one of Shakespeare's many coinages, may mean "surplus" but it also suggests "flux," discharge by the bowels. Whether this shows the heavens to be in any way just seems dubious. A trace of the King's rebel Prometheanism seems to abide.

When the Fool emerges from the hovel, we encounter Edgar's prodigious impersonation of Tom o'Bedlam, carried off with verve and a genius for playacting:

Enter Fool, from the hovel.

Edgar: [*within*] Fathom and half, fathom and half! Poor Tom!

Fool: Come not in here, nuncle, here's a spirit. Help me, help me!

Kent: Give me thy hand. Who's there?

Fool: A spirit, a spirit! He says his name's Poor Tom.

Kent: What art thou that dost grumble there i'the straw? Come forth.

Enter Edgar, disguised as Poor Tom.

Edgar: Away, the foul fiend follows me. Through the sharp hawthorn blows the cold wind. Humh, go to thy cold bed and warm thee.

Lear: Didst thou give all to thy two daughters? And art thou come to this?

act 3, scene 4, lines 39–49

Assimilating Poor Tom to his own situation, it cannot be said that Lear thus crosses the line into madness. One could argue that a hidden element in the King was always a step away from mania, but is that persuasive? The prime element in Lear's personality is his boundless capacity for affect. He needs to love and be loved, yet increasingly he closes himself off from an ability to accept Cordelia's honest reticence. A reverence for her silence would have saved him and her. Some inexplicable flaw blinds him and stops too late to avert tragedy.

> **Edgar:** Who gives anything to Poor Tom? Whom the foul
> fiend hath led through fire and through flame, through
> ford and whirlpool, o'er bog and quagmire; that hath
> laid knives under his pillow and halters in his pew; set
> ratsbane by his porridge, made him proud of heart, to
> ride on a bay trotting horse over four-inched bridges, to
> course his own shadow for a traitor. Bless thy five wits,
> Tom's a-cold. O do, de, do, de, do, de: bless thee from
> whirlwinds, star-blasting, and taking. Do Poor Tom
> some charity, whom the foul fiend vexes. There could
> I have him now, and there, and there again, and there.
> *Storm still.*
>
> act 3, scene 4, lines 50–61

Nothing we have previously encountered in Edgar's nature could have prepared us for this almost surrealist vision. Only a phantom could ride over a bridge one-third of a foot in width. Pursuing his own shadow turned traitor, roaring Mad Tom locates an imagined demon at once within and outside himself. Trans-

muting the storm into whirlwinds that blast an evil influence upon
him, Tom o' Bedlam keeps reaching vainly for his tormentor.

Lear: Have his daughters brought him to this pass?
Couldst thou save nothing? Wouldst thou give 'em all?
Fool: Nay, he reserved a blanket, else we had been all shamed.
Lear: [*to Edgar*] Now all the plagues that in the pendulous air
     Hang fated o'er men's faults light on thy daughters.
Kent: He hath no daughters, sir.
Lear: Death, traitor! Nothing could have subdued nature
To such a lowness but his unkind daughters.
Is it the fashion, that discarded fathers
Should have thus little mercy on their flesh?
Judicious punishment, 'twas this flesh begot
Those pelican daughters.
Edgar: Pillicock sat on Pillicock-Hill,
Alow! Alow, loo, loo!
Fool: This cold night will turn us all to fools and madmen.
Edgar: Take heed o' the foul fiend; obey thy parents, keep thy
     word justly, swear not, commit not with man's sworn spouse,
     set not thy sweet-heart on proud array. Tom's a-cold.
Lear: What hast thou been?
Edgar: A serving-man, proud in heart and mind, that curled
     my hair, wore gloves in my cap, served the lust of my
     mistress' heart and did the act of darkness with her;
     swore as many oaths as I spake words and broke them in
     the sweet face of heaven. One that slept in the contriving
     of lust, and waked to do it. Wine loved I deeply, dice
     dearly; and, in woman, out-paramoured the Turk: false

of heart, light of ear, bloody of hand; hog in sloth, fox in stealth, wolf in greediness, dog in madness, lion in prey. Let not the creaking of shoes, nor the rustling of silks, betray thy poor heart to woman. Keep thy foot out of brothels, thy hand out of plackets, thy pen from lenders' books, and defy the foul fiend. Still through the hawthorn blows the cold wind, says suum, mun, nonny, Dolphin my boy, my boy, *cessez*! Let him trot by.

Storm still.

Lear: Why, thou wert better in a grave than to answer with thy uncovered body this extremity of the skies. Is man no more than this? Consider him well. Thou ow'st the worm no silk, the beast no hide, the sheep no wool, the cat no perfume. Ha? Here's three on's are sophisticated; thou art the thing itself. Unaccommodated man is no more but such a poor, bare, forked animal as thou art. Off, off, you lendings: come, unbutton here.

[*Tearing at his clothes, he is restrained by Kent and the Fool.*]

act 3, scene 4, lines 62–108

Goneril and Regan are pelican daughters since legend holds that the pelican employs its own blood to feed its young. Edgar with dark wit invokes the Pillicock or penis and Pillicock Hill for the mount of Venus. The Fool yields his function to Edgar: "This cold night will turn us all to fools and madmen." In a parody of some of the Ten Commandments, Tom o' Bedlam invents a tale of adultery that prefigures Edmund's amatory escapades with Regan and Goneril. The enemy half brothers retain their occult connection. The chant "False of heart, light of ear, bloody of hand; hog in sloth, fox in stealth, wolf in greediness, dog in madness, lion in prey" was echoed powerfully by Walt Whitman in "Crossing Brooklyn Ferry":

> I am he who knew what it was to be evil,
> I too knitted the old knot of contrariety,
> Blabb'd, blush'd, resented, lied, stole, grudg'd,
> Had guile, anger, lust, hot wishes I dared not speak,
> Was wayward, vain, greedy, shallow, sly, cowardly, malignant,
> The wolf, the snake, the hog, not wanting in me,
> The cheating look, the frivolous word, the adulterous wish, not
>   wanting . . .

Like the singer of the anonymous Tom o' Bedlam song, Edgar imagines a visionary horse whom he names Dauphin, which would have been pronounced "dolphin." In *Henry V*, the heir to the French throne was called Dauphin, since his crest was a dolphin. Lear's response echoes Montaigne's meditation on the misery of man, naked and needing a shroud, borrowed from creatures who possess wool, hair, and feathers, and a dark saying of the Bible:

> What is man, *say I*, that thou art mindful of him? and the son
> of man that thou visitest him?
>
> Geneva Bible, Psalms 8:4

Confronting the disguised Edgar, Lear contrasts Kent, the Fool, and himself as being sophisticated, surprisingly Shakespeare's only use of the word. They are no longer natural; Edgar is the thing itself, unaccommodated man and so unclothed. Magnificently the

Mad King tears at his clothes, so as to join Edgar as the thing itself, but is prevented by Kent and the Fool.

The scene, already pitched so high, ascends to a contrapuntal paroxysm, as the voices of Lear, Edgar, the Fool, and the still rational Kent and Gloucester blend in a harmonious discord:

> **Fool:** Prithee, nuncle, be contented; 'tis a naughty night to
> swim in. Now a little fire in a wild field were like an old
> lecher's heart, a small spark, all the rest on's body cold:
> look, here comes a walking fire.
>
> act 3, scene 4, lines 108–11

The Fool incisively names Gloucester the old lecher, reminding us of the engendering of the Bastard Edmund. Edgar, confronting his father, bursts into a frenzy:

> **Edgar:** This is the foul fiend Flibbertigibbet: he begins at
> curfew and walks till the first cock; he gives the web and
> the pin, squinies the eye and makes the harelip; mildews
> the white wheat and hurts the poor creature of earth.
> Swithold footed thrice the wold;
> He met the nightmare and her nine foal,
> Bid her alight and her troth plight,
> And aroint thee, witch, aroint thee.
>
> act 3, scene 4, lines 112–20

Naming the devil, Poor Tom invents an ominous song fragment in which St. Withold walks to and fro in the upland, and meets the nightmare, a female demon accompanied by her nine foals. The saint compels the nightmare to dismount, to pledge to do no harm, and then he sends her on her way.

Kent: How fares your grace?
Lear: What's he?
Kent: [*to Gloucester*] Who's there? What is't you seek?
Gloucester: What are you there? Your names?
Edgar: Poor Tom, that eats the swimming frog, the toad, the
    tadpole, the wall-newt, and the water—; that in the fury
    of his heart, when the foul fiend rages, eats cow-dung
    for salads; swallows the old rat and the ditch-dog; drinks
    the green mantle of the standing pool; who is whipped
    from tithing to tithing and stocked, punished and
    imprisoned—who hath had three suits to his back, six
    shirts to his body,
        Horse to ride and weapon to wear.
        But mice and rats and such small deer
        Have been Tom's food for seven long year.
    Beware my follower. Peace Smulkin, peace, thou fiend.

act 3, scene 4, lines 121–37

Confronted by his father, Edgar heightens his performance to a horror of suffering and disgust. Smulkin is a minor fiend who appears as a mouse.

Gloucester: What, hath your grace no better company?
Edgar: The prince of darkness is a gentleman. Modo he's
    called, and Mahu.

act 3, scene 4, lines 138–40

For we wrestle not against flesh and blood, but against princi-
palities, against powers, *and* against the worldly governors, *the
princes* of the darkness of this world, against spiritual wickedness, *which are* in the high places.

Geneva Bible, Ephesians 6:12

Modo and Mahu are commanders of the infernal furies. Edgar,
who will bear the final burden of kingship, by implication identifies his struggle against Edmund, Goneril, Regan, and Cornwall with a quest for spiritual virtue. So subtle is Shakespeare that
Edgar's painful development into an avenger who *will* triumph
continues to baffle critical understanding through the ages. The
unwilling restorer of the kingdom comes up through the depths of
degradation at an enormous personal cost.

Gloucester: Our flesh and blood, my lord, is grown so vile
That it doth hate what gets it.

act 3, scene 4, lines 141–42

Poor Gloucester compounds Edgar rather than Edmund with
Goneril and Regan.

Edgar: Poor Tom's a-cold.
Gloucester: [*to Lear*] Go in with me. My duty cannot suffer
T'obey in all your daughters' hard commands.
Though their injunction be to bar my doors
And let this tyrannous night take hold upon you,
Yet have I ventured to come seek you out,
And bring you where both fire and food is ready.
Lear: First let me talk with this philosopher:

[*to Edgar*] What is the cause of thunder?

Kent: Good my lord,

Take his offer, go into the house.

Lear: I'll talk a word with this same learned Theban:

What is your study?

Edgar: How to prevent the fiend and to kill vermin.

Lear: Let me ask you one word in private.

act 3, scene 4, lines 143–56

Thunder, once the voice of the gods to Lear earlier, has now become the enemy. Poignantly, Lear is made to identify Edgar with Diogenes of Thebes, truth-telling Cynic. We do not know the one word Lear wishes to ask, as he is ushered into the refuge.

Kent: [*to Gloucester*] Importune him once more to go, my lord;

His wits begin t'unsettle.

Gloucester: Canst thou blame him?   *Storm still.*

His daughters seek his death. Ah, that good Kent,

He said it would be thus, poor banished man.

Thou sayest the King grows mad; I'll tell thee, friend,

I am almost mad myself. I had a son,

Now outlawed from my blood; he sought my life,

But lately, very late. I loved him, friend,

No father his son dearer. True to tell thee,

The grief hath crazed my wits. What a night's this?

[*to Lear*] I do beseech your grace.

Lear: O, cry you mercy, sir.

[*to Edgar*] Noble philosopher, your company.

Edgar: Tom's a-cold.

Gloucester: In, fellow, there, into the hovel; keep thee warm.

Lear: Come, let's in all.

Kent: This way, my lord.

Lear: With him;
I will keep still with my philosopher.

Kent: Good my lord, soothe him; let him take the fellow.

Gloucester: Take you him on.

Kent: Sirrah, come on; go along with us.

Lear: Come, good Athenian.

Gloucester: No words, no words; hush.

Edgar: Childe Rowland to the dark tower came,
His word was still 'Fie, foh, and fum,
· I smell the blood of a British man.'

act 3, scene 4, lines 157–80

Poor Tom concludes the scene with three remarkable lines, supposedly from a lost ballad but I suspect of Shakespeare's own composition. Robert Browning's magnificent dramatic monologue "Childe Roland to the Dark Tower Came" begins with these lines as epigraph. It is Edgar himself who will become a kind of Roland and destroy the ogre Edmund.

CHAPTER 9

He Childed as I Fathered. / Tom, Away

Edmund descends to the level of Cornwall by betraying Gloucester. Indeed he is in effect adopted by Cornwall. Gloucester, having
rescued Lear and his companions from the storm, departs for the
ordeal that awaits him.

Lear convokes a trial and indicts Goneril and Regan before a
commission of three judges: Edgar, Kent, the Fool:

Lear: Arraign her first, 'tis Goneril—I here take my oath
  before this honourable assembly—kicked the poor King
  her father.
Fool: Come hither, mistress: is your name Goneril?
Lear: She cannot deny it.
Fool: Cry you mercy, I took you for a joint-stool.
Lear: And here's another whose warped looks proclaim
What store her heart is made on. Stop her there!
Arms, arms, sword, fire, corruption in the place!
False justicer, why hast thou let her 'scape?
Edgar: Bless thy five wits.
Kent: O pity! Sir, where is the patience now
That you so oft have boasted to retain?

Edgar: [*aside*] My tears begin to take his part so much
They mar my counterfeiting.

act 3, scene 6, lines 46–60

The madness of his godfather, the King, breaks down Edgar's performative skill. But who would not weep at Lear's pathetic decline?

Lear: The little dogs and all,
Trey, Blanch and Sweet-heart, see, they bark at me.

act 3, scene 6, lines 60–61

Lear's fantasia takes Trey, with its overtones of "betray," as Goneril; Blanch, or "rendering pallid with fright," as Regan; and Sweet-heart as Cordelia.

Lear: Then let them anatomize Regan; see what breeds about
her heart. Is there any cause in nature that makes these
hard hearts?

act 3, scene 6, lines 73–75

Lear literalizes Regan's heartlessness, with a biblical overtone:

He hath blinded their eyes, and hardened their heart, that they should not see with *their* eyes, nor understand with *their* heart, and should be converted, and I should heal them.

Geneva Bible, John 12:40

Lear: [*to Edgar*] You, sir, I entertain you for one of my
hundred; only I do not like the fashion of your garments.

You will say they are Persian attire, but let them be
changed.

Kent: Now, good my lord, lie here and rest awhile.

Lear: Make no noise, make no noise, draw the curtains.

So, so, so; we'll go to supper i'the morning so, so, so.

[*He sleeps.*]

Fool: And I'll go to bed at noon.

act 3, scene 6, lines 75–82

With those words, the Fool vanishes from the play. So does
Tom o' Bedlam. Edgar remains, and will adopt a new disguise.
Lear falls into deep slumber, and is carried off to Dover at the
insistence of Gloucester, who warns that the King's life is in immi-
nent danger. In this most ironic of all tragedies, surpassing even
Hamlet, the cost of Gloucester's decency will be his eyes. There is
a Promethean element in *King Lear,* which inspired a crucial passage in Shelley's *Prometheus Unbound*:

Fury

    In each human heart terror survives
The ravin it has gorged: the loftiest fear
All that they would disdain to think were true:
Hypocrisy and custom make their minds
The fanes of many a worship, now outworn.
They dare not devise good for man's estate,
And yet they know not that they do not dare.
The good want power, but to weep barren tears.
The powerful goodness want: worse need for them.
The wise want love; and those who love want wisdom;
And all best things are thus confused to ill.

Jupiter dispatches his Furies to torment the bound Prometheus. The ultimate Fury sums up the dreadful limitations of the human spirit. The good, lacking power, weep fruitlessly. The powerful, lacking goodness, suffer dearth. The wise, lacking love, and those who love, lacking wisdom, alike are reduced from the best to the worst. William Butler Yeats deliberately echoed Shelley in "The Second Coming":

> Things fall apart; the centre cannot hold;
> Mere anarchy is loosed upon the world,
> The blood-dimmed tide is loosed, and everywhere
> The ceremony of innocence is drowned;
> The best lack all conviction, while the worst
> Are full of passionate intensity.

What Edgar learns to no avail is that:

> The wise want love; and those who love want wisdom.

Shelley's lifelong conviction was that good and the means of good, love and the means of love, were irreconcilable. In this he was Edgar's student:

> **Edgar:** When we our betters see bearing our woes,
> We scarcely think our miseries our foes.
> Who alone suffers, suffers most i'the mind,
> Leaving free things and happy shows behind.
> But then the mind much sufferance doth o'erskip,
> When grief hath mates and bearing fellowship.
> How light and portable my pain seems now,

When that which makes me bend makes the King bow,
He childed as I fathered. Tom, away;
Mark the high noises, and thyself bewray
When false opinion, whose wrong thoughts defile thee,
In thy just proof repeals and reconciles thee.

act 3, scene 6, lines 99–110

Shakespeare invented both "childed" and "fathered." When Edgar cries "He childed as I fathered," I do not think there is any reference to Goneril, Regan, Edmund. Cordelia and Lear, Edgar and Gloucester, are the burden. The recalcitrant yet noble children, and the passionately blind fathers, are bound to the wheel of authentic familial love, which lacks wisdom. The terrible sublimity of *King Lear* rises from this love that is the wisdom of fools, and the folly of the wise.

CHAPTER 10

He That Will Think to Live Till He Be Old, / Give Me Some Help!

The ultimate atrocities represented by Shakespeare are the gouging out of Gloucester's eyes by Cornwall and the hanging of Cordelia. We do not have to endure the sight of Cordelia's immolation, which takes place offstage. But Gloucester's ordeal is enacted before us with graphic verisimilitude.

When Cornwall instructs his servants to apprehend Gloucester, we hear a litany of evil unsurpassed in Shakespeare.

> **Cornwall:** [*to Goneril*] Post speedily to my lord your husband.
>   Show him this letter: the army of France is landed.
>   [*to Servants*] Seek out the traitor, Gloucester.
> **Regan:** Hang him instantly!
> **Goneril:** Pluck out his eyes!
>
> act 3, scene 7, lines 1–5

Characteristically, it is Goneril who enhances the mounting horror.

Cornwall: Leave him to my displeasure. Edmund, keep you
our sister company; the revenges we are bound to take
upon your traitorous father are not fit for your beholding.
Advise the Duke where you are going to a most festinate
preparation; we are bound to the like. Our posts shall
be swift and intelligent betwixt us. Farewell, dear sister;
farewell, my lord of Gloucester.

Enter Oswald.

How now? Where's the King?

Oswald: My lord of Gloucester hath conveyed him hence.
Some five- or six-and-thirty of his knights,
Hot questrists after him, met him at gate,
Who with some other of the lord's dependants
Are gone with him toward Dover, where they boast
To have well-armed friends.

Cornwall: Get horses for your mistress.   *Exit Oswald.*

Goneril: Farewell, sweet lord and sister.

Cornwall: Edmund, farewell.   *Exeunt Goneril and Edmund.*

[*to Servants*] Go seek the traitor Gloucester;
Pinion him like a thief, bring him before us.   *Servants leave.*
Though well we may not pass upon his life
Without the form of justice, yet our power
Shall do a courtesy to our wrath, which men
May blame but not control. Who's there? The traitor?

Enter Gloucester, brought in by two or three Servants.

Regan: Ingrateful fox, 'tis he.

Cornwall: Bind fast his corky arms.

                                        act 3, scene 7, lines 6–29

Gloucester's arms are corky or withered. His age and helplessness are a torment to us.

Gloucester: What means your graces?
Good my friends, consider, you are my guests.
Do me no foul play, friends.
Cornwall: Bind him, I say—
Servants bind his arms.
Regan: Hard, hard. O filthy traitor!
Gloucester: Unmerciful lady as you are, I'm none.
Cornwall: To this chair bind him. [*to Gloucester*] Villain, thou
    shalt find—
Regan plucks his beard.
Gloucester: By the kind gods, 'tis most ignobly done
To pluck me by the beard.

                              act 3, scene 7, lines 29–36

The sadistic plucking at the old man's beard presages Cornwall's plucking out of Gloucester's eyes.

Regan: So white, and such a traitor?
Gloucester: Naughty lady,
These hairs which thou dost ravish from my chin
Will quicken and accuse thee. I am your host;
With robber's hands my hospitable favours
You should not ruffle thus. What will you do?
Cornwall: Come, sir, what letters had you late from France?
Regan: Be simple answered, for we know the truth.

Cornwall: And what confederacy have you with the traitors,
Late footed in the kingdom?
Regan: To whose hands
You have sent the lunatic King. Speak.
Gloucester: I have a letter guessingly set down
Which came from one that's of a neutral heart,
And not from one opposed.
Cornwall: Cunning.
Regan: And false.
Cornwall: Where hast thou sent the King?
Gloucester: To Dover.
Regan: Wherefore to Dover? Wast thou not charged at
     peril—
Cornwall: Wherefore to Dover? Let him first answer that.
Gloucester: I am tied to the stake and I must stand the
     course.

                                   act 3, scene 7, lines 37–53

Shakespeare's playhouse, among others, also accommodated the
Jacobean spectator sport of bear-baiting, in which the wretched
bear was tied to a stake and assaulted by hounds.

Regan: Wherefore to Dover, sir?
Gloucester: Because I would not see thy cruel nails
Pluck out his poor old eyes; nor thy fierce sister
In his anointed flesh stick boarish fangs.
The sea, which such a storm as his bare head
In hell-black night endured, would have buoyed up
And quenched the stelled fires.
Yet, poor old heart, he holp the heavens to rain.

78

If wolves had at thy gate howled that stern time,
Thou shouldst have said, 'Good porter, turn the key,
All cruels else subscribed'; but I shall see
The winged vengeance overtake such children.

act 3, scene 7, lines 54–65

Lear, being royal, had been consecrated with holy oil, another anachronism in this tragedy where so many ages fuse together. The vengeance of the gods does overtake Regan and Goneril, and immediately the monstrous Cornwall, and through the agency of Edgar, Edmund. Gloucester at this moment retains his pagan faith, but I do not think any gods survive the cataclysm that ends this drama.

Cornwall: See't shalt thou never. Fellows, hold the chair;
Upon these eyes of thine I'll set my foot.
Gloucester: He that will think to live till he be old,
Give me some help!—O cruel! O you gods!
Regan: One side will mock another—th'other too.
Cornwall: If you see vengeance—
1st Servant: Hold your hand, my lord.
I have served you ever since I was a child,
But better service have I never done you
Than now to bid you hold.
Regan: How now, you dog?
1st Servant: If you did wear a beard upon your chin,
I'd shake it on this quarrel. What do you mean?
Cornwall: My villein?   *They draw and fight.*
1st Servant: Nay then, come on, and take the chance of anger.

He wounds Cornwall.

Regan: [*to another Servant*] Give me thy sword. A peasant
  stand up thus? *She takes a sword and runs at him behind.*
  Kills him.

1st Servant: O, I am slain. My lord, you have one eye left
To see some mischief on him. O! *He dies.*

Cornwall: Lest it see more, prevent it. Out, vile jelly,
Where is thy lustre now?

Gloucester: All dark and comfortless? Where's my son
  Edmund?
Edmund, enkindle all the sparks of nature
To quit this horrid act.

Regan: Out, treacherous villain,
Thou call'st on him that hates thee. It was he
That made the overture of thy treasons to us,
Who is too good to pity thee.

Gloucester: O my follies! Then Edgar was abused?
Kind gods, forgive me that and prosper him.

Regan: [*to a Servant*] Go, thrust him out at gates and let him
  smell
His way to Dover. How is't, my lord? How look you?

Cornwall: I have received a hurt. Follow me, lady.
[*to Servants*] Turn out that eyeless villain. Throw this slave
Upon the dunghill.
          Exeunt Servants with Gloucester and the body.
          Regan, I bleed apace;
Untimely comes this hurt. Give me your arm.
                    Exeunt Cornwall and Regan.

2nd Servant: I'll never care what wickedness I do
If this man come to good.

3rd Servant: If she live long

And in the end meet the old course of death,
Women will all turn monsters.
2nd Servant: Let's follow the old Earl and get the bedlam
To lead him where he would. His roguish madness
Allows itself to anything.
3rd Servant: Go thou: I'll fetch some flax and whites of eggs
To apply to his bleeding face. Now heaven help him!

act 3, scene 7, lines 66–106

The first servant, though unnamed, redeems humankind by fatally wounding Cornwall. Regan, who will die by poison administered by Goneril, kills the servant with a characteristic stab in the back. I have seen several stage performances of *King Lear*. The gouging of Gloucester's eyes is not to be borne. Why did Shakespeare inflict this scene upon us, and indeed, upon himself?

CHAPTER 11

But That Thy Strange Mutations Make Us Hate Thee, / Life Would Not Yield to Age

The storm is over. In the new day Edgar moves on, a fugitive between disguises, though his array remains Poor Tom's:

> Yet better thus, and known to be contemned,
> Than still contemned and flattered. To be worst,
> The lowest and most dejected thing of fortune,
> Stands still in esperance, lives not in fear.
> The lamentable change is from the best,
> The worst returns to laughter. Welcome then,
> Thou unsubstantial air that I embrace;
> The wretch that thou hast blown unto the worst
> Owes nothing to thy blasts.
> *Enter Gloucester, led by an Old Man.*
> But who comes here?
> My father, parti-eyed? World, world, O world!
> But that thy strange mutations make us hate thee,
> Life would not yield to age.
>
> act 4, scene 1, lines 1–13

It is unclear at what point Edgar realizes his father has been blinded. Yet his mind, like Hamlet's, is quicksilver. Emending "parti-eyed" to "poorly led" is unpersuasive. Edgar, increasingly toughened by his vicissitudes, nevertheless is cast into shock at this sight of Gloucester. I pause here to reconsider some of the enigmas and perplexities evoked by Edgar.

No other major personality in all of Shakespeare has been interpreted as feebly and indeed maliciously as the exemplary Edgar. One critic termed this heroic survivor "a weak and murderous character." More balanced scholars tend to find him unsympathetic and even perverse. As always, my late friend William Elton is the saving exception. He sees Edgar truly as a stubborn triumph of persistence, a pilgrim of filial devotion questing for his ruined father.

Stand back from the vast drama of *King Lear*. Edgar begins as a credulous youth, unaware of evil, and an easy victim for Edmund. Like Kent, he becomes an internal exile, but chooses to go even lower in the social scale than Kent does. As Tom o' Bedlam, Edgar takes the way down and out to the very bottom of societal existence. He startles us with his genius for acting and for enduring.

Edgar mutates from Poor Tom to a disgraced serving man, then to a West Country peasant, then a messenger, and finally to a masked knight in black armor, nameless and fatal, against whom even the formidable Edmund has no chance. In all of Shakespeare, there is nothing like these astonishing metamorphoses.

Edgar the actor, who moves so subtly from disguise to nemesis, has to bear a high cost of transformation. Nothing is got for nothing. Edgar loses his father, his godfather, and his trust in the gods. He gains a kingdom, which he does not want, and is left alone to sustain it when Albany abdicates and Kent prepares to abandon life, somehow to go on serving Lear.

CHAPTER 12

Humanity Must Perforce Prey on Itself, / Like Monsters of the Deep

Blind Gloucester, intending suicide off the cliff at Dover, accepts guidance from the supposed Mad Tom:

Old Man: Alack, sir, you cannot see your way.
Gloucester: I have no way, and therefore want no eyes:
I stumbled when I saw. Full oft 'tis seen
Our means secure us and our mere defects
Prove our commodities. O dear son Edgar,
The food of thy abused father's wrath,
Might I but live to see thee in my touch,
I'd say I had eyes again.
Old Man: How now? Who's there?
Edgar: [*aside*] O gods! Who is't can say 'I am at the worst'?
I am worse than e'er I was.
Old Man: [*to Gloucester*] 'Tis poor mad Tom.
Edgar: [*aside*] And worse I may be yet; the worst is not
So long as we can say, 'This is the worst.'

act 4, scene 1, lines 19–30

The mystery of why Edgar will not reveal his identity to Gloucester may be insoluble. Shakespeare's allusion to Isaiah may be a clue:

Therefore is judgment far from us, neither doth justice come near unto us: we wait for light, but lo, it *is* darkness: for brightness, *but* we walk in darkness.

We grope for the wall like the blind, and we grope as one without eyes: we stumble at the noon day as in the twilight: *we are* in solitary places, as dead men.

Geneva Bible, Isaiah 59:9–10

Edgar also is in darkness. He gropes for the right way to enlighten Gloucester, but even a consciousness as capacious as Hamlet's might be slow to absorb everything that has happened to Edgar and his father.

Old Man: [*to Edgar*] Fellow, where goest?
Gloucester: Is it a beggar-man?
Old Man: Madman, and beggar too.
Gloucester: He has some reason, else he could not beg.
I'the last night's storm I such a fellow saw,
Which made me think a man a worm. My son
Came then into my mind, and yet my mind
Was then scarce friends with him. I have heard more since:
As flies to wanton boys are we to the gods,
They kill us for their sport.

act 4, scene 1, lines 31–39

Gloucester's gods have become vicious children destroying flies for the fun of it. Allusions crowd upon us:

But I am a worm, and not a man: a shame of men, and the contempt of the people.

Geneva Bible, Psalms 22:6

How much more man, a worm, even the son of man, *which is but* a worm?

Geneva Bible, Job 25:6

It is an extraordinary Shakespearean stroke that Gloucester, in gazing upon Mad Tom, had apprehended the human as only a worm, and yet Edgar had entered his thoughts.

Edgar: [*aside*]   How should this be?
Bad is the trade that must play fool to sorrow,
Angering itself and others. [*to Gloucester*] Bless thee, master.

act 4, scene 1, lines 39–41

Returning to acute insight, Edgar reflects not only upon the role he had played as another Fool, but on the darker trade also of Gloucester's intended self-immolation.

Gloucester: Is that the naked fellow?
Old Man: Ay, my lord.
Gloucester: Then prithee get thee away. If for my sake
Thou wilt o'ertake us hence a mile or twain
I'the way toward Dover, do it for ancient love,
And bring some covering for this naked soul,
Which I'll entreat to lead me.
Old Man: Alack, sir, he is mad.
Gloucester: 'Tis the time's plague when madmen lead the blind.

Do as I bid thee, or rather do thy pleasure;
Above the rest, be gone.
Old Man: I'll bring him the best 'pparel that I have,
Come on't what will.   *Exit.*
Gloucester: Sirrah, naked fellow.
Edgar: Poor Tom's a-cold. [*aside*] I cannot daub it further—
                              act 4, scene 1, lines 42–55

I prefer the Quarto version: "I cannot dance it farther," rather than the Folio's "daub," not just because of the play on "father," but since it indicates the exhaustion of Mad Tom's gyrations.

Gloucester: Come hither, fellow.
Edgar: [*aside*] And yet I must. [*to Gloucester*] Bless thy sweet
    eyes, they bleed.
Gloucester: Knowst thou the way to Dover?
Edgar: Both stile and gate, horseway and footpath. Poor
    Tom hath been scared out of his good wits. Bless thee,
    goodman's son, from the foul fiend. Five fiends have been
    in Poor Tom at once, of lust, as Obidicut; Hobbididence,
    prince of darkness; Mahu, of stealing; Modo, of murder;
    Flibbertigibbet, of mopping and mowing, who since
    possesses chambermaids and waiting-women. So, bless
    thee, master.
Gloucester: Here, take this purse, thou whom the heavens'
    plagues
Have humbled to all strokes. That I am wretched
Makes thee the happier. Heavens, deal so still!
Let the superfluous and lust-dieted man
That slaves your ordinance, that will not see

Because he does not feel, feel your power quickly:
So distribution should undo excess
And each man have enough. Dost thou know Dover?
Edgar: Ay, master.
Gloucester: There is a cliff whose high and bending head
Looks fearfully in the confined deep:
Bring me but to the very brim of it,
And I'll repair the misery thou dost bear
With something rich about me. From that place
I shall no leading need.
Edgar: Give me thy arm,
Poor Tom shall lead thee.

act 4, scene 1, lines 56–82

We return to the vexed question of Edgar's delay in identifying himself to his father. Healing despair is an impossible enterprise, and who among us would do better than Edgar? There is also the possibility that Edgar's immersion in demonology, though play-acting, has activated a daemon in himself. Demons are devils, but the daemon is one's Genius, and takes over one's personality.

Goneril and Edmund then enter, with the wretched Oswald following them in:

Goneril: Welcome, my lord. I marvel our mild husband
Not met us on the way. [*to Oswald*] Now, where's your master?
Oswald: Madam, within; but never man so changed.
I told him of the army that was landed;
He smiled at it. I told him you were coming;
His answer was 'The worse.' Of Gloucester's treachery
And of the loyal service of his son,

When I informed him, then he called me sot,
And told me I had turned the wrong side out.
What most he should dislike seems pleasant to him,
What like, offensive.

act 4, scene 2, lines 1–11

Goneril is mistaken in terming Albany "mild." Slow to rouse, he now proves fierce and dangerous to her.

Goneril: [*to Edmund*] Then shall you go no further.
It is the cowish terror of his spirit,
That dares not undertake. He'll not feel wrongs
Which tie him to an answer. Our wishes on the way
May prove effects. Back, Edmund, to my brother;
Hasten his musters and conduct his powers.
I must change names at home and give the distaff
Into my husband's hands. This trusty servant
Shall pass between us. Ere long you are like to hear—
If you dare venture in your own behalf—
A mistress's command. Wear this.
            [*She places a chain around his neck.*]
                              Spare speech,
Decline your head. This kiss, if it durst speak,
Would stretch thy spirits up into the air.
Conceive, and fare thee well—
Edmund: Yours in the ranks of death.   *Exit.*
Goneril: —my most dear Gloucester.
O, the difference of man and man!
To thee a woman's services are due;

A fool usurps my bed.

Oswald: Madam, here comes my lord.

act 4, scene 2, lines 11–29

Absurdly mistaken, Goneril cannot apprehend Albany's outrage. To her, Albany is a woman and should spin flax on the distaff. She will take up the sword. Her plot to murder Albany begins. Edmund is to replace him. His gallant "Yours in the ranks of death" will be prophetic for both of them and for her rival Regan.

Enter Albany.

Goneril: I have been worth the whistling.

Albany: O Goneril,
You are not worth the dust which the rude wind
Blows in your face. I fear your disposition;
That nature which contemns its origin
Cannot be bordered certain in itself.
She that herself will sliver and disbranch
From her material sap perforce must wither,
And come to deadly use.

Goneril: No more, the text is foolish.

Albany: Wisdom and goodness to the vile seem vile;
Filths savour but themselves. What have you done?
Tigers, not daughters, what have you performed?
A father, and a gracious aged man
Whose reverence even the head-lugged bear would lick,
Most barbarous, most degenerate, have you madded.
Could my good brother suffer you to do it?
A man, a prince, by him so benefitted?

If that the heavens do not their visible spirits
Send quickly down to tame these vile offences,
It will come:
Humanity must perforce prey on itself,
Like monsters of the deep.

act 4, scene 2, lines 30–51

We wince at the unintended irony of terming the slain Cornwall "my good brother." The visible spirits are the daemons or heavenly messengers, which is one of Edgar's roles, as Albany cannot know. "Daemons" here means personal angels, guided by the will. Goneril and Regan are monsters of the deep, preying upon their victims, and at last on each other.

Goneril: Milk-livered man,
That bear'st a cheek for blows, a head for wrongs,
Who hast not in thy brows an eye discerning
Thine honour from thy suffering; that not knowst
Fools do those villains pity who are punished
Ere they have done their mischief. Where's thy drum?
France spreads his banners in our noiseless land;
With plumed helm thy state begins to threat,
Whilst thou, a moral fool, sits still and cries,
'Alack, why does he so?'
Albany: See thyself, devil:
Proper deformity shows not in the fiend
So horrid as in woman.
Goneril: O vain fool!
Albany: Thou changed and self-covered thing, for shame
Be-monster not thy feature. Were't my fitness

To let these hands obey my blood,
They are apt enough to dislocate and tear
Thy flesh and bones. Howe'er thou art a fiend,
A woman's shape doth shield thee.
Goneril: Marry, your manhood, mew!—

act 4, scene 2, lines 51–69

One could wish that Albany had yielded to his proper instinct and torn Goneril apart, then and there. A catcall is her reply, even as a messenger arrives:

Enter a Messenger.
Albany: What news?
Messenger: O my good lord, the Duke of Cornwall's dead,
Slain by his servant, going to put out
The other eye of Gloucester.
Albany: Gloucester's eyes?
Messenger: A servant that he bred, thrilled with remorse,
Opposed against the act, bending his sword
To his great master, who, thereat enraged,
Flew on him, and amongst them felled him dead;
But not without that harmful stroke which since
Hath plucked him after.
Albany: This shows you are above,
You justicers, that these our nether crimes
So speedily can venge. But, O, poor Gloucester,
Lost he his other eye?
Messenger: Both, both, my lord.
[*to Goneril*] This letter, madam, craves a speedy answer;
'Tis from your sister.

Goneril: [*aside*]   One way I like this well;
But being widow, and my Gloucester with her,
May all the building in my fancy pluck
Upon my hateful life. Another way,
The news is not so tart.
[*to the Messenger*]   I'll read and answer.

                              act 4, scene 2, lines 70–88

Goneril's mixed reaction is revelatory. Cornwall's death weakens Regan, but frees her to annex Edmund. Yet Goneril's fancy or ambitious dream house of possessing both Edmund and the kingdom smashes down and returns to the reality of her hatred for Albany.

Albany: Where was his son when they did take his eyes?
Messenger: Come with my lady hither.
Albany: He is not here.
Messenger: No, my good lord; I met him back again.
Albany: Knows he the wickedness?
Messenger: Ay, my good lord; 'twas he informed against him
And quit the house on purpose that their punishment
Might have the freer course.
Albany: Gloucester, I live
To thank thee for the love thou showd'st the King
And to revenge thine eyes. Come hither, friend,
Tell me what more thou knowst.

                              act 4, scene 2, lines 89–98

Albany, who will have to compromise that revenge in order to meet the French invasion led by Cordelia, becomes a third with

Kent and Edgar. Their mutual mission is to rescue Lear and punish the malefactors. And yet the perplexities of Albany's situation at last will culminate in his abdication, in favor of Edgar. The monsters of the deep do not triumph, and still the best cannot abide by their convictions. Albany has to defend Britain against invasion, though that means he must fight against Cordelia. Kent, seeking only to serve Lear, cannot reach him in time. Edgar, struggling into heroism, is baffled by his own ambivalences. And so, all best things are thus confused to ill.

CHAPTER 13

O Ruined Piece of Nature, This Great World / Shall So Wear Out to Naught

The disguised Kent encounters a Gentleman whose description of Cordelia as loving daughter permanently sets our judgment of her:

Kent: Why the King of France is so suddenly gone back, know you no reason?

Gentleman: Something he left imperfect in the state which since his coming forth is thought of, which imports to the kingdom so much fear and danger that his personal return was most required and necessary.

Kent: Who hath he left behind him General?

Gentleman: The Marshal of France, Monsieur la Far.

Kent: Did your letters pierce the queen to any demonstration of grief?

Gentleman: Ay, sir. She took them, read them in my presence, And now and then an ample tear trilled down Her delicate cheek. It seemed she was a queen Over her passion, who, most rebel-like,

Sought to be king o'er her.

Kent: O, then it moved her?

Gentleman: Not to a rage; patience and sorrow strove

Who should express her goodliest. You have seen

Sunshine and rain at once, her smiles and tears

Were like a better way. Those happy smilets,

That played on her ripe lip seemed not to know

What guests were in her eyes, which parted thence

As pearls from diamonds dropped. In brief,

Sorrow would be a rarity most beloved

If all could so become it.

act 4, scene 3, lines 1–24

Some critics judge this description of Cordelia to be over-wrought, yet it comes as a blessed relief after so much terror. As a loving child, Cordelia more than contrasts with Goneril and Regan. Her mingled tears and smiles anticipate Lear's and Gloucester's in their later scenes of recognition and reconciliation. Like them, she incarnates love, but she is free of Lear's excessiveness, and of Gloucester's anxious expectations.

Kent: Made she no verbal question?

Gentleman: Faith, once or twice she heaved the name of father

Pantingly forth as if it pressed her heart;

Cried 'Sisters, sisters, shame of ladies, sisters!

Kent, father, sisters! What, i'the storm, i'the night?

Let pity not be believed!' There she shook

The holy water from her heavenly eyes,

And clamour mastered her; then away she started,

To deal with grief alone.

Kent: It is the stars,
The stars above us govern our conditions,
Else one self mate and make could not beget
Such different issues. You spoke not with her since?
Gentleman: No.
Kent: Was this before the King returned?
Gentleman: No, since.
Kent: Well, sir, the poor distressed Lear's i'the town,
Who sometime in his better tune remembers
What we are come about, and by no means
Will yield to see his daughter.
Gentleman: Why, good sir?
Kent: A sovereign shame so elbows him. His own unkindness
That stripped her from his benediction, turned her
To foreign casualties, gave her dear rights
To his dog-hearted daughters, these things sting
His mind so venomously that burning shame
Detains him from Cordelia.

act 4, scene 3, lines 25–48

That is a new Lear, purged of fury and on the verge of a renewed sanity. We might not have thought him capable of remorse, but now self-recognition burgeons and with it the realization of much that was lacking.

Gentleman: Alack, poor gentleman.
Kent: Of Albany's and Cornwall's powers you heard not?
Gentleman: 'Tis so; they are afoot.
Kent: Well, sir, I'll bring you to our master, Lear,

And leave you to attend him. Some dear cause
Will in concealment wrap me up awhile.
When I am known aright, you shall not grieve,
Lending me this acquaintance.
I pray you, go along with me.

act 4, scene 3, lines 48–56

We are not told the nature of that "dear cause." I surmise that, like Edgar, Kent keeps to disguise because a restoration of identity will involve enormous energies that have been repressed for too long. Continuous acting, night and day, exhausts the spirit, unless your gift for it is extraordinary. Kent is less damaged by his impersonations than Edgar, but then the self-abasement of a nobleman becoming his King's body-servant is of a different sphere from a descent into the degradation of a mad beggar. Down in the depths of his inmost being, Edgar has encountered a new personality, his own and yet unknown to him. He strives to keep up with this transformation, yet its exfoliation escapes his apprehension.

The Earl of Kent can be puzzling. His absolute devotion to Lear consumes his entire being. In that sense he resembles Horatio and, like Hamlet's faithful companion, he sometimes serves the function of a chorus. Both Kent and Horatio subdue themselves to their love for the King or for the Prince. Kent and Horatio are figures of mediation. The audience cannot access instantly the vastness of Lear's emotions, just as the capaciousness of Hamlet's consciousness defeats our understanding. It may be that Kent and Horatio alike stand for our uncertain presence in the world of tragedy, where total immersion might destroy us. Something in all of us defends our everyday existence from Shakespeare's onslaught of feelings. Thoughts of such intensity so throng us that we are in danger of inundation. Relentless and vehement, Shakespeare's images do not allow us to interpose a little ease. We need release, and it is denied us.

There is no relief for us from the high tragedy of Lear. Cordelia and her French forces enter in search of the wild old King:

> *Enter with drum and colours, Cordelia, Gentleman, Officer and*
> *soldiers.*
> **Cordelia:** Alack, 'tis he. Why, he was met even now
> As mad as the vexed sea, singing aloud,
> Crowned with rank fumiter and furrow-weeds,
> With burdocks, hemlock, nettles, cuckoo-flowers,
> Darnel and all the idle weeds that grow
> In our sustaining corn. [*to Officer*] A century send forth;
> Search every acre in the high-grown field
> And bring him to our eye.
>
> > act 4, scene 4, lines 1–8

Few visions, even in Shakespeare, are as sublime as the great King, mad as the sea, singing aloud, and self-crowned with the flowers and weeds of an English summer.

> **Cordelia:**   What can man's wisdom
> In the restoring his bereaved sense,
> He that helps him take all my outward worth.
> **Gentleman:** There is means, madam.
> Our foster nurse of nature is repose,
> The which he lacks: that to provoke in him
> Are many simples operative, whose power
> Will close the eye of anguish.

Cordelia: All blest secrets,
All you unpublished virtues of the earth,
Spring with my tears. Be aidant and remediate
In the good man's distress. Seek, seek for him,
Lest his ungoverned rage dissolve the life
That wants the means to lead it.

act 4, scene 4, lines 8–19

To be "aidant and remediate" is to aid and remedy. And so, Cordelia yearns for a cure that will return her father from madness.

Enter a Messenger.
Messenger: News, madam:
The British powers are marching hitherward.
Cordelia: 'Tis known before. Our preparation stands
In expectation of them. O dear father,
It is thy business that I go about;

act 4, scene 4, lines 19–23

Then said he unto them, How is it that ye sought me? knew ye not that I must go about my Father's business?

Geneva Bible, Luke 2:49

The allusion to Jesus is unmistakable yet deliberately misleading. Cordelia and her troops are there for battle, so as to assert again Lear's right to the throne. Jesus is abandoning his parents, to go about Yahweh's affairs in the Jerusalem Temple. The play is profuse with biblical echoes, but they are not oriented to a Christian interpretation. Virtually every version of Christianity is addicted to hope, though that fulfillment is not for this world. *The Tragedy of King Lear* leaps beyond hope, into nothingness. The promised end becomes an image of horror and the emblematic motto is "Fall and Cease!"

Cordelia: Therefore great France
My mourning and important tears hath pitied.
No blown ambition doth our arms incite,
But love, dear love, and our aged father's right:
Soon may I hear and see him.

act 4, scene 4, lines 25–29

"Important" probably should be "importuned," as it is in the Folio. Cordelia is passionately sincere, but it is hardly Christian to say that love, rather than puffed-up ambition, stimulates the good to battle.

Oswald bears Regan a letter from Goneril, and a note from Goneril to Edmund:

Regan: But are my brother's powers set forth?
Oswald: Ay, madam.
Regan: Himself in person there?
Oswald: Madam, with much ado; your sister is the better
    soldier.
Regan: Lord Edmund spake not with your lord at home?
Oswald: No, madam.
Regan: What might import my sister's letter to him?
Oswald: I know not, lady.
Regan: Faith, he is posted hence on serious matter.
It was great ignorance, Gloucester's eyes being out,
To let him live. Where he arrives he moves

All hearts against us. Edmund, I think, is gone,
In pity of his misery, to dispatch
His nighted life; moreover to descry
The strength o'th' enemy.

act 4, scene 5, lines 1–16

Regan, true to herself, suggests that Edmund, out of pity for his father, will finish the good work by murdering the blind old man.

Oswald: I must needs after him, madam, with my letter.
Regan: Our troops set forth tomorrow; stay with us.
The ways are dangerous.
Oswald: I may not, madam;
My lady charged my duty in this business.
Regan: Why should she write to Edmund? Might not you
Transport her purposes by word? Belike—
Some things, I know not what—I'll love thee much;
Let me unseal the letter.
Oswald: Madam, I had rather—
Regan: I know your lady does not love her husband,
I am sure of that; and at her late being here
She gave strange oeillades and most speaking looks
To noble Edmund. I know you are of her bosom.
Oswald: I, madam?
Regan: I speak in understanding: y'are, I know't.
Therefore I do advise you take this note.
My lord is dead; Edmund and I have talked,
And more convenient is he for my hand
Than for your lady's. You may gather more.

If you do find him, pray you give him this;
And when your mistress hears thus much from you,
I pray desire her call her wisdom to her.
So fare you well.
If you do chance to hear of that blind traitor,
Preferment falls on him that cuts him off.
Oswald: Would I could meet him, madam, I should show
What party I do follow.
Regan: Fare thee well.

                                    act 4, scene 5, lines 17–43

"Oeillades" are lustful glances. Cornwall's death is dismissed and Regan pursues her own lustful quest. It is some satisfaction to the audience that Oswald soon will be cudgeled to death by Edgar, defending his helpless father.

Now disguised as a peasant, Edgar leads Gloucester to what is supposed to be Dover Cliff, from which the blind father intends to hurl himself into the sea. Something all but inscrutable in Edgar animates his desperate attempt to cure his despairing father from the design of suicide. Is it that the exhaustions of disguise render Edgar ripe for this risky therapy? Or can it be that simulating Tom o' Bedlam's derangement has disturbed Edgar's perilous balance?

Gloucester: When shall I come to the top of that same hill?
Edgar: You do climb up it now. Look how we labour.
Gloucester: Methinks the ground is even.
Edgar: Horrible steep.
Hark, do you hear the sea?

                                    act 4, scene 6, lines 1–4

Keats composed his sonnet "On the Sea" at the prompting of Edgar's deceptive "Hark, do you hear the sea?"

Gloucester: No, truly.
Edgar: Why then your other senses grow imperfect
By your eyes' anguish.
Gloucester: So may it be indeed.
Methinks thy voice is altered, and thou speak'st
In better phrase and matter than thou didst.
Edgar: You're much deceived; in nothing am I changed
But in my garments.
Gloucester: Methinks you're better spoken.
Edgar: Come on, sir, here's the place. Stand still: how fearful
And dizzy 'tis, to cast one's eyes so low.
The crows and choughs that wing the midway air
Show scarce so gross as beetles. Half-way down
Hangs one that gathers samphire, dreadful trade;
Methinks he seems no bigger than his head.
The fishermen that walk upon the beach
Appear like mice, and yond tall anchoring barque
Diminished to her cock, her cock a buoy
Almost too small for sight. The murmuring surge,
That on th' unnumb'red idle pebble chafes,
Cannot be heard so high. I'll look no more,
Lest my brain turn, and the deficient sight
Topple down headlong.
Gloucester: Set me where you stand.
Edgar: Give me your hand: you are now within a foot
Of th'extreme verge. For all beneath the moon

Would I not leap upright.
Gloucester: Let go my hand.
Here, friend,'s another purse, in it a jewel
Well worth a poor man's taking. Fairies and gods
Prosper it with thee! Go thou further off;
Bid me farewell and let me hear thee going.
Edgar: Now fare ye well, good sir.
Gloucester: With all my heart.
Edgar: [*aside*] Why I do trifle thus with his despair
Is done to cure it.

                                        act 4, scene 6, lines 4–34

To unravel Edgar's motivation you need to give up various scholarly opinions that accuse him of cruelty. He is neither weak nor sadistic. Love for his father torments him. It is the essence of tragedy in this terrifying drama that love breaks and deforms.

Gloucester: [*He kneels.*] O you mighty gods,
This world I do renounce and in your sights
Shake patiently my great affliction off.
If I could bear it longer and not fall
To quarrel with your great opposeless wills,
My snuff and loathed part of nature should
Burn itself out. If Edgar live, O, bless him!
Now, fellow, fare thee well.   *He falls.*

                                        act 4, scene 6, lines 34–41

The blessing on Edgar is crucial but not yet sufficient to arm him for the struggle ahead. His dilemmas are caught with exquisite precision in the poem by James Agee dedicated to the photographer Walker Evans:

> Against time and the damages of the brain
> Sharpen and calibrate. Not yet in full,
> Yet in some arbitrated part
> Order the façade of the listless summer.
>
> Spies, moving delicately among the enemy,
> The younger sons, the fools,
> Set somewhat aside the dialects and the stained skins of feigned
>   madness,
> Ambiguously signal, baffle, the eluded sentinel.
>
> Edgar, weeping for pity, to the shelf of that sick bluff,
> Bring your blind father, and describe a little;
> Behold him, part wakened, fallen among field flowers shallow
> But undisclosed, withdraw.
>
> Not yet that naked hour when armed,
> Disguise flung flat, squarely we challenge the fiend.
> Still, comrade, the running of beasts and the ruining heaven
> Still captive the old wild king.

The phrasing in Agee's poem is close to inevitable, and its burden abounds in poignance and insight. "Sharpen," "calibrate," and "arbitrated" provide a rugged consonance, an accord or idea of order that delineates Edgar's design of disguises. After the mock suicide, Edgar withdraws undisclosed. Why? We keep coming back to that dark query. Agee deftly suggests that Edgar works against time. He waits patiently for that naked hour of self-revelation when he will arm himself and challenge the fiend Edmund. Edgar, our comrade, must still endure the bestial running of Goneril and Regan, and the heaven that cares only for ruining us. The old wild Lear always will be still captive, above all of the gods themselves.

Blind Gloucester falls, invoking the gods to witness his renunciation of life. Shakespeare's design, already complex, elaborates yet more variations in Edgar's consciousness:

Edgar: Gone, sir; farewell.
[*aside*] And yet I know not how conceit may rob
The treasury of life when life itself
Yields to the theft. Had he been where he thought,
By this had thought been past. [*to Gloucester*] Alive or dead?
Ho, you, sir! Friend, hear you, sir? Speak!—
[*aside*] Thus might he pass indeed. Yet he revives.—
What are you, sir?
Gloucester: Away and let me die.

                              act 4, scene 6, lines 41–48

"Conceit" or imagination might itself kill Gloucester and rob him of "the treasury of life." We value Edgar for affirming that the only wealth is life, and for not resting from mental fight until his reluctant acceptance of the burden of kingship.

Edgar: Hadst thou been aught but gossamer, feathers, air,
So many fathom down precipitating,
Thou'dst shivered like an egg; but thou dost breathe,

109

Hast heavy substance, bleed'st not, speak'st, art sound.
Ten masts at each make not the altitude
Which thou hast perpendicularly fell.
Thy life's a miracle. Speak yet again.

In Edgar's purged vision, all of life is a miracle.

Gloucester: But have I fallen, or no?
Edgar: From the dread summit of this chalky bourn.
Look up a-height: the shrill-gorged lark so far
Cannot be seen or heard. Do but look up.
Gloucester: Alack, I have no eyes.
Is wretchedness deprived that benefit
To end itself by death? 'Twas yet some comfort
When misery could beguile the tyrant's rage,
And frustrate his proud will.
Edgar: Give me your arm.
Up, so. How is't? Feel you your legs? You stand.
Gloucester: Too well, too well.
Edgar: This is above all strangeness.
Upon the crown o'the cliff what thing was that
Which parted from you?
Gloucester: A poor unfortunate beggar.
Edgar: As I stood here below, methought his eyes
Were two full moons. He had a thousand noses,
Horns whelked and waved like the enraged sea.
It was some fiend. Therefore, thou happy father,
Think that the clearest gods, who make them honours
Of men's impossibilities, have preserved thee.

                              act 4, scene 6, lines 49–74

Assuming yet another voice, he reassures his father. Tom o' Bedlam vanishes in Edgar's extravagant vision of a fiend exorcized by the faultless gods who have saved Gloucester.

Gloucester: I do remember now. Henceforth I'll bear
Affliction till it do cry out itself
'Enough, enough,' and die. That thing you speak of,
I took it for a man. Often 'twould say,
'The fiend, the fiend'; he led me to that place.
Edgar: Bear free and patient thoughts.

act 4, scene 6, lines 75–80

Poor Gloucester is being asked to be like the Christian God, plainly impossible in this desolation. Yet Edgar remains desperate to preserve his father, though still reluctant to divulge his true identity. Edgar has a foreboding that the revelation itself could destroy Gloucester, as it will before the avenging son goes forth to slay Edmund.

What follows seems to me the supreme achievement in all of Shakespeare, and perhaps of Western literature. In one hundred lines that do not advance the plot, mad Lear and blind Gloucester confront each other, with Edgar as despairing chorus:

Enter Lear mad, crowned with wild flowers.
Edgar: But who comes here?
The safer sense will ne'er accommodate
His master thus.
Lear: No, they cannot touch me for coining. I am the King
himself.
Edgar: O thou side-piercing sight!

act 4, scene 6, lines 80–85

Edgar beholds his King and godfather insanely wreathed. Sight, the safer sense, cannot absorb the spectacle. In this nihilistic play, riddled with Christian allusions, Edgar's heart is rent and we hear John 19:34:

But one of the soldiers with a spear pierced his side, and forthwith came there out blood and water.

Geneva Bible

Lear: Nature's above art in that respect. There's your press-money. That fellow handles his bow like a crow-keeper: draw me a clothier's yard. Look, look, a mouse: peace, peace, this piece of toasted cheese will do't. There's my gauntlet, I'll prove it on a giant. Bring up the brown bills. O, well flown, bird, i'the clout, i'the clout! Hewgh! Give the word.
Edgar: Sweet marjoram.
Lear: Pass.

Thrown back to his days as battle leader, mad Lear demands the password and Edgar aptly replies "Sweet marjoram," a remedy for diseases of the brain.

Gloucester: I know that voice.
Lear: Ha! Goneril with a white beard? They flattered me like a dog and told me I had the white hairs in my beard ere the black ones were there. To say 'ay' and 'no' to everything that I said 'ay' and 'no' to was no good divinity. When the rain came to wet me once and the wind to make me chatter; when the thunder would not peace at

my bidding, there I found 'em, there I smelt 'em out. Go
to, they are not men o'their words: they told me I was
everything; 'tis a lie, I am not ague-proof.

act 4, scene 6, lines 86–104

For sixty years of his reign, Lear's flatterers told him he was
everything in himself, but he has learned he is nothing. Wor-
shipped as a god, he fears a fall from man to outcast wretch.

Gloucester: The trick of that voice I do well remember:
Is't not the King?
Lear: Ay, every inch a king.
When I do stare, see how the subject quakes.
I pardon that man's life. What was thy cause?
Adultery?
Thou shalt not die—die for adultery? No!
The wren goes to't and the small gilded fly
Does lecher in my sight. Let copulation thrive,
For Gloucester's bastard son was kinder to his father
Than my daughters got 'tween the lawful sheets.
To't, luxury, pell-mell, for I lack soldiers.
Behold yon simp'ring dame,
Whose face between her forks presages snow,
That minces virtue and does shake the head
To hear of pleasure's name—
The fitchew, nor the soiled horse, goes to't with a more riotous
	appetite. Down from the waist they are centaurs, though
	women all above. But to the girdle do the gods inherit,
	beneath is all the fiend's: there's hell, there's darkness,
	there is the sulphurous pit, burning, scalding, stench,

consumption! Fie, fie, fie! Pah, pah! Give me an ounce
of civet, good apothecary, to sweeten my imagination.
There's money for thee.

act 4, scene 6, lines 105–27

Even in his distress, Lear recoils from his own misogyny and
equation of the vagina with hell, a slang word in Shakespeare's day
for the female genitals. He appeals to blind Gloucester as if he
were a pharmacist, and seeks to purchase civet or musky perfume.

Gloucester: O, let me kiss that hand!
Lear: Let me wipe it first, it smells of mortality.
Gloucester: O ruined piece of nature, this great world
Shall so wear out to naught. Dost thou know me?
Lear: I remember thine eyes well enough. Dost thou squiny at
me? No, do thy worst, blind Cupid, I'll not love.
Read thou this challenge, mark but the penning of it.
Gloucester: Were all thy letters suns, I could not see one.

act 4, scene 6, lines 128–36

It is not that Lear again recoils from the stench of female sexu-
ality. His bitterness is universal. The human is reduced to deathli-
ness, whether man or woman. When Gloucester cries out that his
great King is a ruined piece of nature, it may be that the "piece" is
both an apocalyptic fragment and the masterpiece of our world—
having been father, god, king—wearing out to nothingness.

Unintentionally cruel, mad Lear associates Gloucester's blindness with Cupid's, and the afflicted Earl breaks our hearts, as he
does Edgar's, with his dignified, "Were all thy letters suns, I could
not see one."

Edgar: [*aside*] I would not take this from report; it is,
And my heart breaks at it.
Lear: Read.
Gloucester: What? With the case of eyes?
Lear: O ho, are you there with me? No eyes in your head, nor
    no money in your purse? Your eyes are in a heavy case,
    your purse in a light, yet you see how this world goes.
Gloucester: I see it feelingly.

Again Gloucester speaks to and for all of us. How can one read
or attend this drama without seeing feelingly?

Lear: What, art mad? A man may see how this world goes
    with no eyes. Look with thine ears. See how yon justice
    rails upon yon simple thief. Hark in thine ear: change
    places and handy-dandy, which is the justice, which is the
    thief? Thou hast seen a farmer's dog bark at a beggar?
Gloucester: Ay, sir.
Lear: And the creature run from the cur—there thou mightst
    behold the great image of authority: a dog's obeyed in
    office.

act 4, scene 6, lines 137–55

Lear indeed is the great image of authority, but Shakespeare
subverts authority in this vision of a dog who is obeyed in office.

Lear: Thou, rascal beadle, hold thy bloody hand;
Why dost thou lash that whore? Strip thy own back,
Thou hotly lusts to use her in that kind
For which thou whipp'st her. The usurer hangs the cozener.

Through tattered clothes great vices do appear;
Robes and furred gowns hide all. Plate sin with gold,
And the strong lance of justice hurtless breaks;
Arm it in rags, a pigmy's straw does pierce it.
None does offend, none, I say none. I'll able 'em;
Take that of me, my friend, who have the power
To seal th'accuser's lips. Get thee glass eyes,
And like a scurvy politician seem
To see the things thou dost not. Now, now, now, now,
Pull off my boots; harder, harder, so.
Edgar: [*aside*] O matter and impertinency mixed,
Reason in madness.

act 4, scene 6, lines 156–71

How could one better Edgar's judgment of reason in madness? Shakespeare rushes us on to revelation by way of an extraordinary transformation of biblical wisdom. I myself am haunted by Shakespeare's identification of Lear with Solomon the Wise, who reigned for a half century and then suffered the sorrows of extreme old age:

Lear: If thou wilt weep my fortunes, take my eyes.
I know thee well enough, thy name is Gloucester.
Thou must be patient. We came crying hither:
Thou knowst the first time that we smell the air
We wawl and cry. I will preach to thee: mark me.
Gloucester: Alack, alack the day!
Lear: When we are born we cry that we are come
To this great stage of fools.

act 4, scene 6, lines 172–79

Lear echoes the Wisdom of Solomon:

I my selfe also am a mortall man, like to all, and the ofspring of
    him that was first made of the earth,
And in my mothers wombe was fashioned to be flesh in the
    time of tenne moneths being compacted in blood, of the
    seed of man, and the pleasure that came with sleepe.
And when I was borne, I drew in the common aire, and fell
    upon the earth which is of like nature, and the first voice
    which I uttered, was crying as all others doe.
I was nursed in swadling clothes, and that with cares.
For there is no king that had any other beginning of birth.
For all men have one entrance unto life, and the like going out.
          Geneva Bible, Wisdom of Solomon 7:1–6

Lear is very conscious that he is now only playing the part of
the King, and he devastates by associating the cry of birth with the
great stage of fools or victims upon which all of us perform. All
the world is a platform for apocalypse. The gods rain down mis-
fortunes upon us all, whether great kings or ordinary mortals. And
we all fall face forward fighting on the stage, unable to save either
ourselves or our dear ones.

Lear's full madness returns. When Cordelia's messengers
attempt to rescue him, he flees:

Gentleman: O, here he is: lay hand upon him. Sir,
Your most dear daughter—
Lear: No rescue? What, a prisoner? I am even
The natural fool of fortune. Use me well,
You shall have ransom. Let me have surgeons,

I am cut to the brains.

Gentleman: You shall have anything.

Lear: No seconds? All myself?

Why, this would make a man a man of salt,

To use his eyes for garden water-pots.

Ay, and laying autumn's dust.

Gentleman: Good sir.

Lear: I will die bravely, like a smug bridegroom.

What? I will be jovial. Come, come,

I am a king, my masters, know you that?

Gentleman: You are a royal one, and we obey you.

Lear: Then there's life in't. Come, an you get it,

You shall get it by running. Sa, sa, sa, sa.

act 4, scene 6, lines 184–99

Terming himself the natural fool of fortune, and so a fool since birth, Lear gallantly insists he will die courageously like a bridegroom, attired for the sexual fulfillment of marriage. The King speeds off, calling out "sa, sa, sa, sa," a hunting cry.

Gloucester, led off by Edgar in the latest of his disguises, a peasant of the West Country, is reconciled to a natural death. In another of the drama's endless ironies, the minor brute Oswald enters with drawn sword, intending to cut down the blind man:

Oswald: A proclaimed prize! Most happy!

That eyeless head of thine was first framed flesh

To raise my fortunes! Thou old unhappy traitor,

Briefly thyself remember. The sword is out

That must destroy thee.

Gloucester: Now let thy friendly hand

Put strength enough to't.

Oswald: Wherefore, bold peasant,
Dar'st thou support a published traitor? Hence,
Lest that th'infection of his fortune take
Like hold on thee. Let go his arm.

Edgar: Ch'ill not let go, zir, without vurther 'cagion.

Oswald: Let go, slave, or thou diest.

Edgar: Good gentleman, go your gait and let poor voke pass.
      And 'ch'ud ha' been zwaggered out of my life, 'twould not
      ha' been zo long as 'tis by a vortnight. Nay, come not near
      th'old man; keep out, che vor ye, or I'se try whether your
      costard or my baton be the harder. Ch'ill be plain with you.

Oswald: Out, dunghill.   *Draws his sword. They fight.*

Edgar: Ch'ill pick your teeth, zir. Come, no matter vor your
      foins. [*Oswald falls.*]

Oswald: Slave, thou hast slain me. Villain, take my purse.
If ever thou wilt thrive, bury my body,
And give the letters which thou find'st about me
To Edmund, Earl of Gloucester. Seek him out
Upon the English party. O untimely death, death!   *He dies.*

Edgar: I know thee well; a serviceable villain,
As duteous to the vices of thy mistress
As badness would desire.

Gloucester: What, is he dead?

                              act 4, scene 6, lines 223–49

One admires Edgar's ability to assume yet another accent. The horrible Oswald wields sword against Edgar's cudgel, and receives his proper quietus. Goneril's letter to Edmund is uncovered, activating a nemesis that will destroy both of them and Regan:

119

Edgar: Sit you down, father; rest you.—
Let's see these pockets: the letters that he speaks of
May be my friends. He's dead; I am only sorry
He had no other deathsman. Let us see:
Leave, gentle wax; and manners, blame us not.
To know our enemies' minds we rip their hearts,
Their papers is more lawful.
[*Reads the letter.*] 'Let our reciprocal vows be remembered. You
    have many opportunities to cut him off. If your will want
    not, time and place will be fruitfully offered. There is
    nothing done if he return the conqueror; then am I the
    prisoner, and his bed my gaol, from the loathed warmth
    whereof, deliver me and supply the place for your labour.
    Your (wife, so I would say) affectionate servant and for
    you her own for venture. Goneril.'
O indistinguished space of woman's will!
A plot upon her virtuous husband's life
And the exchange my brother. Here in the sands
Thee I'll rake up, the post unsanctified
Of murderous lechers; and in the mature time,
With this ungracious paper strike the sight
Of the death-practised duke. For him 'tis well
That of thy death and business I can tell. [*Exit dragging the
    body.*]
Gloucester: The King is mad; how stiff is my vile sense,
That I stand up and have ingenious feeling
Of my huge sorrows? Better I were distract;
So should my thoughts be severed from my griefs,
And woes by wrong imaginations lose
The knowledge of themselves.   *Drum afar off.*

Edgar: Give me your hand.
Far off methinks I hear the beaten drum.
Come, father, I'll bestow you with a friend.

                              act 4, scene 6, lines 250–81

This extraordinary scene concludes with the emergence of yet another Edgar, the just and rational avenger who sees what is to be done and will do it. Shakespeare must have realized a certain trailing off of force after Lear runs off, but such a diminishment was necessary. Edgar is augmented, not diminished, and we move with him toward finalities.

CHAPTER 14

Thou Art a Soul in Bliss, But I Am Bound / Upon a Wheel of Fire

Shakespeare adroitly juxtaposes Edgar's disposal of Oswald with the reunion of Cordelia and Kent:

> **Cordelia:** O thou good Kent, how shall I live and work
> To match thy goodness? My life will be too short,
> And every measure fail me.

The cruel irony is that Cordelia's life will be too short indeed, and her benign measures will fail her.

> **Kent:** To be acknowledged, madam, is o'erpaid.
> All my reports go with the modest truth,
> Nor more nor clipped, but so.
> **Cordelia:**   Be better suited;
> These weeds are memories of those worser hours.
> I prithee put them off.
> **Kent:**   Pardon, dear madam;
> Yet to be known shortens my made intent.

My boon I make it, that you know me not
Till time and I think meet.
Cordelia: Then be't so, my good lord.

act 4, scene 7, lines 1-12

Kent can be as puzzling as Edgar, yet not in so fine a tone. Why does he maintain his disguise? Perhaps, but this is surmise, Shakespeare intended a final recognition scene between Lear and Kent. It will not take place. This is akin to his not portraying the moment when Edgar identifies himself to Gloucester and asks his blessing. Edgar narrates that piercing final revelation. Shakespeare may have decided that Kent and Edgar alike might distract from the reunion of Lear and Cordelia, and from the great King's entry with the dead child cradled in his arms.

Lear wakes to find Cordelia:

Cordelia: How does my royal lord? How fares your majesty?
Lear: You do me wrong to take me out o'the grave.
Thou art a soul in bliss, but I am bound
Upon a wheel of fire that mine own tears
Do scald like molten lead.
Cordelia: Sir, do you know me?
Lear: You are a spirit, I know; where did you die?

act 4, scene 7, lines 44–49

William Elton notes that the "wheel of fire" is a syncretic vision, fusing several traditions. Lear refers to the myth of Ixion, King of Thessaly, who murdered his father-in-law and became an insane outcast. Zeus, out of pity, took Ixion and gave him a place in Olympus, where he lusted after Hera. In revenge, Zeus fabricated

124

a false Hera as a cloud. Ixion fornicated with this simulacrum and a son, Centauros, was born. Pindar tells us that Centauros cohabited with the Magnesian mares on Mount Pelion and produced the race of Centaurs.

Zeus blasted Ixion with lightning, threw him out of Olympus, and had Hermes bind him to a wheel of fire perpetually spinning. The ancient British tradition of Beltane marked the advent of summer by a festival in which wheels of fire were rolled down hillsides. For five thousand years the spoked solar wheel was seen as the attribute of the chariot of the sun. Lear's wheel of fire is thus both Celtic and Classical, as well as a new version of the wheel of fortune.

Initially Lear mistakes Cordelia for a heavenly being, and wonders where this spirit died. Realization comes to him:

Where have I been? Where am I? Fair daylight?
I am mightily abused. I should ev'n die with pity
To see another thus. I know not what to say.
I will not swear these are my hands: let's see—
I feel this pinprick. Would I were assured
Of my condition.

Fearful of deception, the King lacks all conviction and yet returns to sanity:

Cordelia: [*Kneels.*] O look upon me, sir,
And hold your hands in benediction o'er me!
No, sir, you must not kneel.
Lear: Pray do not mock me.
I am a very foolish, fond old man,
Fourscore and upward, not an hour more nor less;

And to deal plainly,
I fear I am not in my perfect mind.
Methinks I should know you and know this man,
Yet I am doubtful: for I am mainly ignorant
What place this is and all the skill I have
Remembers not these garments; nor I know not
Where I did lodge last night. Do not laugh at me,
For, as I am a man, I think this lady
To be my child Cordelia.
Cordelia: And so I am, I am.
Lear: Be your tears wet? Yes, faith; I pray weep not.
If you have poison for me, I will drink it.
I know you do not love me, for your sisters
Have, as I do remember, done me wrong.
You have some cause, they have not.
Cordelia: No cause, no cause.
Lear: Am I in France?
Kent: In your own kingdom, sir.
Lear: Do not abuse me.

                              act 4, scene 7, lines 52–77

We are at one of the limits of art. Even Shakespeare never sur-
passed this. The love of daughter and father achieves absolute
expression. I cannot think of another place in Western literature
that is so luminous and poignant. Shakespeare himself has other
reunions, in *Pericles* and *The Winter's Tale*, that move us with the
startled joy of familial reconciliations. Yet even they do not equal
this.

Aristotle emphasized that the tragic hero can achieve a recognition (anagnorisis—"knowing again" or "knowing back" or

"knowing throughout") in which he experiences "a change from ignorance to awareness of a bond of love or hate." I sometimes think that all of Shakespeare moves toward a recognition scene, one that would be total and transcendent. Perhaps he never quite gets there, but this blessed moment between Lear and Cordelia comes closest.

Cordelia leads Lear away. Kent closes this sublime scene with a mysterious couplet:

My point and period will be throughly wrought,
Or well or ill, as this day's battle's fought.

act 4, scene 7, lines 95–96

It may be that Kent looks forward to a moment of completion in which his life will be fulfilled by reconciliation with Lear. If that is so, Shakespeare gives us yet another dark irony.

CHAPTER 15

Men Must Endure / Their Going Hence Even as Their Coming Hither. / Ripeness Is All

The final act of the tragedy begins with the forces of Edmund and Regan awaiting the arrival of Albany, Goneril, and their troops:

> Edmund: [*to a Gentleman*] Know of the Duke if his last
>   purpose hold,
> Or whether since he is advised by aught
> To change the course. He's full of alteration
> And self-reproving. Bring his constant pleasure.

Albany, riven by doubts, is desperately divided between his devotion to Lear and his British patriotism in confronting a French invasion.

> Regan: Our sister's man is certainly miscarried.
> Edmund: 'Tis to be doubted, madam.

The slain Oswald, as Edmund fears, will not be found again.

Regan: Now, sweet lord,
You know the goodness I intend upon you:
Tell me but truly, but then speak the truth,
Do you not love my sister?
Edmund: In honoured love.
Regan: But have you never found my brother's way
To the forfended place?
Edmund: That thought abuses you.
Regan: I am doubtful that you have been conjunct
And bosomed with her, as far as we call hers.
Edmund: No, by mine honour, madam.
Regan: I never shall endure her. Dear my lord,
Be not familiar with her.
Edmund: Fear me not.
                           act 5, scene 1, lines 1–17

Regan has offered herself to Edmund as royal bride. She accurately apprehends that the Bastard is their shared lover. His chilled denial is not persuasive. The entry of Goneril, Albany, and their host augments the murderous tension between the fatal sisters. In the decisive moment of the entire tragedy, Edgar, in his peasant disguise, approaches Albany:

Edgar: If e'er your grace had speech with man so poor,
Hear me one word.
Albany: [*to his soldiers*] I'll overtake you.
                       [*to Edgar*] Speak.

Edgar: Before you fight the battle, ope this letter.
If you have victory, let the trumpet sound
For him that brought it. Wretched though I seem,
I can produce a champion that will prove
What is avouched there. If you miscarry,
Your business of the world hath so an end
And machination ceases. Fortune love you.
Albany: Stay till I have read the letter.
Edgar: I was forbid it.
When time shall serve, let but the herald cry
And I'll appear again.
Albany: Why, fare thee well. I will o'erlook thy paper.

                                   act 5, scene 1, lines 38–51

The letter from Goneril to Edmund proposes the murder of
Albany. Its revelation will destroy Regan, Goneril, and Edmund,
in that order. In his final soliloquy, Edmund both surpasses himself
and knowingly begins to touch a limit:

To both these sisters have I sworn my love,
Each jealous of the other as the stung
Are of the adder. Which of them shall I take?
Both? One? Or neither? Neither can be enjoyed
If both remain alive. To take the widow
Exasperates, makes mad her sister Goneril,
And hardly shall I carry out my side,
Her husband being alive. Now then, we'll use
His countenance for the battle, which being done,
Let her who would be rid of him devise

His speedy taking off. As for the mercy
Which he intends to Lear and to Cordelia,
The battle done, and they within our power,
Shall never see his pardon; for my state
Stands on me to defend, not to debate.

act 5, scene 1, lines 56–70

There is an outrageous charm in his "Which of them shall I take? / Both? One? Or neither?" We can be daunted by the prospect of a double date with Goneril and Regan, but we are not Edmund. He cheerfully expects Albany's extinction by Goneril, and prophesies the execution of Cordelia, and of Lear, who thwarts the plot but too late.

After the French defeat, Edgar rescues his reluctant father for a last time:

Edgar: Away, old man, give me thy hand, away!
King Lear hath lost, he and his daughter ta'en.
Give me thy hand; come on!
Gloucester: No further, sir; a man may rot even here.
Edgar: What, in ill thoughts again? Men must endure
Their going hence even as their coming hither.
Ripeness is all. Come on.
Gloucester: And that's true too.

act 5, scene 2, lines 5–12

There's a touch of Hamlet in Edgar when he intones:

> Men must endure
Their going hence even as their coming hither.
Ripeness is all.

Again William Elton is the best guide. He shows that "Ripeness is all" is a Renaissance commonplace. The image of "ripeness" fits pagan naturalism as much as it does Christian hope. The Stoic sense of enduring sorrows with resignation is at least as dominant as the Christian vision of divinely ordained completion. John Keats, in his great ode "To Autumn," meditates upon Edgar's word:

> Season of mists and mellow fruitfulness,
>   Close bosom-friend of the maturing sun;
> Conspiring with him how to load and bless
>   With fruit the vines that round the thatch-eves run;
> To bend with apples the moss'd cottage-trees,
>   And fill all fruit with ripeness to the core;

Keats, no Christian, accurately and sensitively caught the stoic naturalism of Edgar's stance.

CHAPTER 16

The Gods Are Just
and of Our Pleasant Vices /
Make Instruments
to Plague Us

All of us are so moved by the loving reunion of Lear and Cordelia that we are falsely tempted to the hope that, in spite of their terrible victimization, somehow they will survive in this apocalyptic drama. Charles Lamb, a great Romantic critic, in his *On the Tragedies of Shakespeare* (1812), eloquently dismissed such wistful longings:

> A happy ending! as if the living martyrdom that Lear had gone through, the flaying of his feelings alive, did not make a fair dismissal from the stage of life the only decorous thing for him. If he is to live and be happy after, if he could sustain this world's burden after, why all this pudder and preparation, why torment us with all this unnecessary sympathy? As if the childish pleasure of getting his gilt robes and sceptre again could tempt him to act over again his misused station, as if at his years, and with his experience, any thing was left but to die.
>
> Lear is essentially impossible to be represented on a stage.

Is the play now beyond us? The great King and Edgar defeat meditation. You can brood endlessly on Falstaff, Hamlet, Cleopatra, Iago, and Macbeth, but not on Lear and Edgar, who transcend the limits of thought. Their actions and sufferings hint that human travail is meaningless.

The ultimate ordeal of Lear and Cordelia ensues directly from the sadism of Edmund:

Edmund: Some officers take them away—good guard,
Until their greater pleasures first be known
That are to censure them.
Cordelia: We are not the first
Who with best meaning have incurred the worst.
For thee, oppressed King, I am cast down;
Myself could else outfrown false fortune's frown.
Shall we not see these daughters and these sisters?
Lear: No, no, no, no. Come let's away to prison;
We two alone will sing like birds i'the cage.
When thou dost ask me blessing I'll kneel down
And ask of thee forgiveness. So we'll live
And pray, and sing, and tell old tales, and laugh
At gilded butterflies, and hear poor rogues
Talk of court news; and we'll talk with them too—
Who loses and who wins, who's in, who's out—
And take upon's the mystery of things
As if we were God's spies. And we'll wear out
In a walled prison packs and sects of great ones
That ebb and flow by the moon.

                                        act 5, scene 3, lines 1–19

What is it to take upon us the mystery of things? There is a defiant presumption in that bold enterprise. We hear an overtone of:

For the mystery of iniquity doth already work: only he which now withholdeth, *shall let* till he be taken out of the way.

Geneva Bible, Thessalonians 2:7

"God's spies" are daemons who go to and fro on the earth, serving the pagan gods. William Elton reads this as bordering on blasphemy, which I find persuasive. Lear, whose universe is now entirely Cordelia, achieves a final desperate balance before the hanging of his child.

Edmund: Take them away.
Lear: Upon such sacrifices, my Cordelia,
The gods themselves throw incense. Have I caught thee?
   [*Embraces her.*]
He that parts us shall bring a brand from heaven,
And fire us hence like foxes. Wipe thine eyes;
The good-years shall devour them, flesh and fell,
Ere they shall make us weep!
We'll see 'em starved first: come.

Exeunt Lear and Cordelia guarded.
act 5, scene 3, lines 19–26

It is astonishing that the pagan King, joyously embracing his lost daughter, should mix biblical overtones into the drama's syncretic religion:

And Samson went out, and took three hundred foxes, and took firebrands, and turned them tail to tail, and put a firebrand in the midst between two tails.

And when he had set the brands on fire, he sent them out into the standing corn of the Philistines, and burnt up both the ricks and the standing corn, with the vineyards *and* olives.

Geneva Bible, Judges 15:4–5

And two years after, Pharaoh also dreamed, and behold, he stood by a river.

And lo, there came out of the river seven goodly kine and fat-fleshed, and they fed in a meadow.

And lo, seven other kine came up after them out of the river, evil favored and lean fleshed, and stood by the *other* kine upon the brink of the river.

And the evil favored and lean fleshed kine did eat up the seven well favored and fat kine: so Pharaoh awoke.

Again he slept, and dreamed the second time: and behold, seven ears of corn grew upon one stalk, rank and goodly.

And lo, seven thin ears, and blasted with the East wind, sprang up after them.

Geneva Bible, Genesis 41:1–6

Regarding Cordelia and Lear as sacrifices welcomed by the gods with incense is a fearful vista. Samson, burning up the Philistine fields with firebrands tied to foxes' tails, is analogized to heaven's firebrand burning up Edmund, Goneril, Regan. Pharaoh's dream, interpreted by Joseph, becomes a forlorn image of Lear's illusive hope that good years with Cordelia await him. Instead Edmund's instruction to murder them will be the reality.

From now until the end, Edmund plays out his doom, aware of what impends:

Flourish. Enter Albany, Goneril, Regan, and soldiers with a Trumpeter.
Albany: Sir, you have showed today your valiant strain
And fortune led you well. You have the captives
Who were the opposites of this day's strife:
I do require them of you, so to use them
As we shall find their merits and our safety
May equally determine.

                            act 5, scene 3, lines 41–46

Albany's design is deep and dangerous for Edmund, as he well knows. Asserting his authority, Albany demands Lear and Cordelia as his own prisoners.

Edmund: Sir, I thought it fit
To send the old and miserable King
To some retention and appointed guard,
Whose age had charms in it, whose title more,
To pluck the common bosom on his side,
And turn our impressed lances in our eyes
Which do command them. With him I sent the queen,
My reason all the same; and they are ready
Tomorrow, or at further space, t'appear
Where you shall hold your session. At this time
We sweat and bleed; the friend hath lost his friend

And the best quarrels in the heat are cursed
By those that feel their sharpness.
The question of Cordelia and her father
Requires a fitter place.

"A fitter place" provokes Albany's assertion of command and a reduction of Edmund to a mere subject.

Albany: Sir, by your patience,
I hold you but a subject of this war,
Not as a brother.
Regan: That's as we list to grace him.
Methinks our pleasure might have been demanded
Ere you had spoke so far. He led our powers,
Bore the commission of my place and person,
The which immediacy may well stand up
And call itself your brother.

Regan is quick-witted enough but her scolding is vain.

Goneril: Not so hot!
In his own grace he doth exalt himself
More than in your addition.
Regan: In my rights,
By me invested, he compeers the best.
Albany: That were the most, if he should husband you.
Regan: Jesters do oft prove prophets.
Goneril: Holla, holla!
That eye that told you so looked but asquint.

                    act 5, scene 3, lines 46–73

Jealous love proverbially renders an eye asquint. Here there is a reverberation of Regan urging Cornwall to pluck out both of Gloucester's eyes.

Regan: Lady, I am not well, else I should answer
From a full-flowing stomach. [*to Edmund*] General,
Take thou my soldiers, prisoners, patrimony;
Dispose of them, of me, the walls is thine.
Witness the world, that I create thee here
My lord and master.

Poisoned by Goneril, Regan manages this grandiose proclamation, as empty as it will prove fatal.

Goneril: Mean you to enjoy him then?
Albany: The let-alone lies not in your good will.
Edmund: Nor in thine, lord.
Albany: Half-blooded fellow, yes.
Regan: [*to Edmund*] Let the drum strike and prove my title
    thine.

                              act 5, scene 3, lines 74–82

Albany's controlled fury mounts up to a challenge while insulting Edmund as a bastard. Regan's last defiance will ebb soon enough into the sickness of death.

Albany: Stay yet, hear reason: Edmund, I arrest thee
On capital treason, and in thine attaint
This gilded serpent.   *Points to Goneril.*
[*to Regan*]   For your claim, fair sister,

141

I bar it in the interest of my wife:
'Tis she is sub-contracted to this lord
And I her husband contradict your banns:
If you will marry, make your loves to me;
My lady is bespoke.

act 5, scene 3, lines 83–90

With an ironic power that is new to him, Albany both charges
Edmund with treason and dismisses Goneril with bitter contempt.
Perhaps the only comic moment in the drama is ventured by Albany's invitation to Edmund that points to the outrageousness of the
situation.

Goneril: An interlude!
Albany: Thou art armed, Gloucester. Let the trumpet sound.
If none appear to prove upon thy person
Thy heinous, manifest and many treasons,
There is my pledge.   *Throws down his gauntlet.*
                 I'll make it on thy heart,
Ere I taste bread, thou art in nothing less
Than I have here proclaimed thee.
Regan: Sick, O, sick!
Goneril: [*aside*] If not, I'll ne'er trust medicine.
Edmund: There's my exchange.   *Throws down his gauntlet.*
                      What in the world he is
That names me traitor, villain-like he lies.
Call by the trumpet: he that dares approach,
On him, on you—who not?—I will maintain
My truth and honour firmly.
Albany: A herald, ho!

Enter a Herald.

[*to Edmund*] Trust to thy single virtue, for thy soldiers,
All levied in my name, have in my name
Took their discharge.

act 5, scene 3, lines 90–105

Despite his bravado, Edmund well knows he is finished. His army disbanded, even if he were to slay Albany or the unknown challenger, he would perish. Perhaps he wears down or has become doom-eager.

Regan: My sickness grows upon me.
Albany: She is not well; convey her to my tent. *Exit Regan.*
Come hither, herald; let the trumpet sound
And read out this. *A trumpet sounds.*
Herald: [*Reads.*] 'If any man of quality or degree within the
lists of the army will maintain upon Edmund, supposed
Earl of Gloucester, that he is a manifold traitor, let him
appear by the third sound of the trumpet. He is bold in
his defense.' *First trumpet.*
Again! *Second trumpet.*
Again! *Third trumpet.*
Trumpet answers within.
Enter Edgar armed.
Albany: Ask him his purposes, why he appears
Upon this call o'the trumpet.
Herald: What are you?
Your name, your quality, and why you answer
This present summons?
Edgar: O know my name is lost,

143

By treason's tooth bare-gnawn and canker-bit;
Yet am I noble as the adversary
I come to cope withal.

act 5, scene 3, lines 105–22

A master of disguises and of assumed voices, Edgar at last has become himself. Evidently he is masked, and sports no coat of arms. I suggest that he has returned to his own voice, and that Edmund has to recognize him.

Albany: Which is that adversary?
Edgar: What's he that speaks for Edmund, Earl of Gloucester?
Edmund: Himself. What say'st thou to him?
Edgar: Draw thy sword,
That if my speech offend a noble heart,
Thy arm may do thee justice. Here is mine. [*Draws his sword.*]
Behold: it is the privilege of mine honours,
My oath, and my profession. I protest,
Maugre thy strength, youth, place, and eminence,
Despite thy victor sword and fire-new fortune,
Thy valour, and thy heart, thou art a traitor:
False to thy gods, thy brother and thy father,
Conspirant 'gainst this high illustrious prince,
And from th' extremest upward of thy head
To the descent and dust below thy foot
A most toad-spotted traitor. Say thou no,
This sword, this arm and my best spirits are bent
To prove upon thy heart, whereto I speak,
Thou liest.

act 5, scene 3, lines 122–39

A legitimate pride, for the first time, fires Edgar's challenge. After his purgatorial pilgrimage, Gloucester's true son takes up the stance of the destined avenger. His language is a rush of precise heroism focused upon belated justice.

> **Edmund:** In wisdom I should ask thy name,
> But since thy outside looks so fair and warlike,
> And that thy tongue some say of breeding breathes,
> What safe and nicely I might well delay
> By rule of knighthood, I disdain and spurn.
> Back do I toss these treasons to thy head,
> With the hell-hated lie o'erwhelm thy heart,
> Which for they yet glance by and scarcely bruise,
> This sword of mine shall give them instant way,
> Where they shall rest forever. Trumpets, speak.
> *Alarums. They fight. Edmund falls.*
>
> act 5, scene 3, lines 139–48

When Edmund cites wisdom, formally he is correct, since an unknown antagonist could be a hired sword. I do not think the Bastard indulges in softness or even manifests hubris. He may suspect he faces his brother and he accepts the fiction of the masked knight's disguise. Though there is a stage tradition that prolongs the duel, an imaginative director would keep it brief and deadly. Edmund has no chance.

> **Albany:** Save him, save him!

Albany urges Edgar not to finish, so that Edmund can be questioned.

Goneril: This is mere practice, Gloucester.
By the law of war thou wast not bound to answer
An unknown opposite. Thou art not vanquished,
But cozened and beguiled.

Goneril, her world falling apart, insists Edmund is the victim of an assassination, but he has been his own assassin, almost from the moment we first encounter him.

Albany: Shut your mouth, dame,
Or with this paper shall I stop it.
[*to Edmund*]   Hold, sir,
Thou worse than any name, read thine own evil.
[*to Goneril*] Nay, no tearing, lady; I perceive you know it.
Goneril: Say if I do, the laws are mine, not thine.
Who can arraign me for't?
Albany: Most monstrous! O!
[*to Edmund*] Knowst thou this paper?
Edmund: Ask me not what I know.
                    act 5, scene 3, lines 149–58

Edmund speaks this in the Folio, Goneril in the Quarto. The line is more powerful coming from Edmund, since it marks the start of his unexpected change.

Albany: [*to an officer, who follows Goneril*]
Go after her; she's desperate, govern her.
Edmund: What you have charged me with, that have I done,
And more, much more; the time will bring it out.

146

'Tis past and so am I. [*to Edgar*] But what art thou
That hast this fortune on me? If thou'rt noble,
I do forgive thee.

It is a weak reading to interpret Edmund as lapsing into con-
ventional ideas of nobility. He accepts the wheel of fortune but
wishes Edgar to make explicit what both of them know.

Edgar: Let's exchange charity:
I am no less in blood than thou art, Edmund;
If more, the more thou'st wronged me.
My name is Edgar and thy father's son.

Removing the mask, Edgar reveals himself in a line of singular
resonance:

My name is Edgar and thy father's son.

After a fugitive purgatory, Edgar reclaims his name. The stroke is
the more puissant by saying *thy* father's son, rather than *my* father's son.

The gods are just and of our pleasant vices
Make instruments to plague us:
The dark and vicious place where thee he got
Cost him his eyes.

                              act 5, scene 3, lines 159–71

I can never stop hearing those four lines. They commit Edgar
to a fierce morality in which all of us are the fools of time. But I

wince at Edgar's description of the vagina as "the dark and vicious place." Since Edmund abandoned his father to Cornwall's barbarism, Edgar's point is true enough. Yet the heroism that developed in Edgar has come at a high cost, turning him away from sexual life.

There are so very many other costs. Like Hamlet, Edgar has seen into the abyss of our reality, and discovered it to be nothing. Edgar's pilgrimage is from innocence through experience into nihilism. Browning's narrator in "Childe Roland to the Dark Tower Came" is the direct descendant of Edgar. There is no ogre waiting for Browning's quester at the Dark Tower. All that you confront there is yourself, and the lost adventurers, your peers, who arrived there before you. After a life spent training for the sight, you cannot at first recognize it, because you have overprepared the event.

What does Edgar accomplish? He rids the earth of Edmund and Oswald, a major and a minor fiend. But his quest is for reconciliation with his father, Gloucester, and his godfather, Lear. He achieves the first, only to see his father die of mixed grief and joy. He sees the final entrance of Lear, who bears the dead Cordelia in his arms. And then Lear, too, dies of joy and grief.

Edmund: Thou'st spoken right, 'tis true;
The wheel is come full circle, I am here.

           act 5, scene 3, lines 171–72

The wheel of fortune and Lear's wheel of fire come together. Edmund's conclusion is carried by the simple fact of a dying man upon the ground.

The recognition scene of Edgar and Albany is revelatory in several senses. Stretched beyond limits, Edgar expresses the terror of the human condition, in which we hold on to life even when something in us dies hour by hour. Blaming himself for recalcitrance, Edgar cannot cast out remorse:

Albany: Where have you hid yourself?
How have you known the miseries of your father?
Edgar: By nursing them, my lord. List a brief tale,
And when 'tis told, O, that my heart would burst!
The bloody proclamation to escape
That followed me so near—O, our lives' sweetness,
That we the pain of death would hourly die
Rather than die at once!—taught me to shift
Into a madman's rags, t'assume a semblance
That very dogs disdained; and in this habit
Met I my father with his bleeding rings,
Their precious stones new lost; became his guide,
Led him, begged for him, saved him from despair,
Never—O fault!—revealed myself unto him
Until some half-hour past, when I was armed,
Not sure, though hoping of this good success.
I asked his blessing and from first to last
Told him our pilgrimage. But his flawed heart,
Alack, too weak the conflict to support,
'Twixt two extremes of passion, joy and grief,
Burst smilingly.

act 5, scene 3, lines 178–98

The question of that "fault" is the question of Edgar. Was the delayed revelation a matter of personal recalcitrance? Or was it indeed a flaw in Edgar? Many scholars are quick to blame him, but I am not of their company. I have come to believe that Edgar, rightly or wrongly, felt he did not merit his father's blessing until he was armed for vengeance. There is also the son's realization that his father was at the limit of endurance, and revelation might kill him. Gloucester suffers a fatal heart attack as the rival passions of joy at his son's restoration and grief at his own earlier injustice assault him.

Is it the role of Edgar to be a pilgrim of hope? Shakespeare knew better and so should we. Edgar is an uncelebrated hero of the negative way, no other being available in this great drama.

CHAPTER 17

We That Are Young /
Shall Never See So Much,
nor Live So Long

The final movement of *King Lear* can be said to begin with the startling change in the dying Edmund:

> **Edmund:**   This speech of yours hath moved me,
> And shall perchance do good; but speak you on,
> You look as you had something more to say.

"Moved" and "good" ring strangely when coming from Edmund. And yet he ebbs toward a reversal he will not live to attain.

> **Albany:** If there be more, more woeful, hold it in,
> For I am almost ready to dissolve
> Hearing of this.
> **Edgar:**   This would have seemed a period
> To such as love not sorrow, but another
> To amplify too much would make much more
> And top extremity.

Whilst I was big in clamour, came there in a man
Who, having seen me in my worst estate,
Shunned my abhorred society, but then finding
Who 'twas that so endured, with his strong arms,
He fastened on my neck and bellowed out
As he'd burst heaven, threw him on my father,
Told the most piteous tale of Lear and him
That ever ear received, which in recounting
His grief grew puissant and the strings of life
Began to crack. Twice then the trumpets sounded
And there I left him tranced.
Albany: But who was this?
Edgar: Kent, sir, the banished Kent, who in disguise
Followed his enemy king and did him service
Improper for a slave.

                              act 5, scene 3, lines 198–220

Kent very nearly becomes a third victim with Gloucester and
Lear. In grief he throws himself on Gloucester's corpse, caught
between sleep and waking. Edgar cannot stay to comfort him, as
the third blast of the trumpet impends.

Enter a Gentleman with a bloody knife.
Gentleman: Help, help, O, help!
Edgar: What kind of help?
Albany: Speak, man.
Edgar: What means this bloody knife?
Gentleman: 'Tis hot, it smokes,
It came even from the heart of—O, she's dead!
Albany: Who dead? Speak, man.

Albany's question turns upon the proleptic possibility that Cordelia is dead, and that will prove true soon enough.

Gentleman: Your lady, sir, your lady; and her sister
By her is poisoned; she confesses it.
Edmund: I was contracted to them both; all three
Now marry in an instant.

act 5, scene 3, lines 221–28

Edmund, who had pledged himself outrageously to both Goneril and Regan—"Yours in the ranks of death"—now fulfills his vow by preparing to die with both his mistresses.

Edgar: Here comes Kent.
Enter Kent.
Albany: Produce the bodies, be they alive or dead.
Goneril's and Regan's bodies brought out.
This judgement of the heavens, that makes us tremble
Touches us not with pity—O, is this he?
The time will not allow the compliment
Which very manners urges.
Kent: I am come
To bid my King and master aye good night.
Is he not here?
Albany: Great thing of us forgot!
Speak, Edmund, where's the King? And where's
     Cordelia?
Seest thou this object, Kent?
Kent: Alack, why thus?
Edmund: Yet Edmund was beloved:

153

The one the other poisoned for my sake,
And after slew herself.
Albany: Even so; cover their faces.

In a remarkable moment of self-overhearing, Edmund will react to this realization: "Yet Edmund *was* beloved." No matter that what he calls "love" was the lust for him of two monsters of the deep. That sense of having been connected turns him around. He sees that he also is one of the fools of time, victims of themselves.

Edmund: I pant for life. Some good I mean to do,
Despite of mine own nature. Quickly send—
Be brief in it—to the castle, for my writ
Is on the life of Lear and on Cordelia;
Nay, send in time.
Albany: Run, run, O run.
Edgar: To who, my lord? Who has the office? [*to Edmund*]
      Send
Thy token of reprieve.
Edmund: Well thought on, take my sword; the captain,
Give it the captain.
Edgar: [*to Gentleman*] Haste thee for thy life.
Edmund: He hath commission from thy wife and me
To hang Cordelia in the prison and
To lay the blame upon her own despair,
That she fordid herself.
Albany: The gods defend her. Bear him hence awhile.
Edmund is carried off.
                              act 5, scene 3, lines 228–54

Nearing death, Edmund states a final opposition between "good" and "nature." That severance, characteristic of his entire life, comes apart in dying. In a final irony, Edmund is carried off to die out of our sight. He will not know whether Cordelia survives. I always wonder who he thought he was, as he lay dying. Did he feel vindicated at having stood up for his bastardy? I doubt that he thought about Gloucester, the father he had betrayed. It is unlikely that Edgar was in his mind, since the brothers had exchanged forgiveness. Goneril and Regan would have vanished away, except as memories of his sexual prowess. Perhaps he returned to his praise of nature as his goddess.

In what must be the shattering beyond all measure, in Shakespeare and indeed all Western literature, Lear enters with the dead Cordelia in his arms:

Lear: Howl, howl, howl, howl! O, you are men of stones!
Had I your tongues and eyes, I'd use them so
That heaven's vault should crack: she's gone for ever.
I know when one is dead and when one lives;
She's dead as earth.   *He lays her down.*
                    Lend me a looking-glass;
If that her breath will mist or stain the stone,
Why then she lives.

That fourfold "howl" is the cry of the human in Lear, and an injunction to all of us to shout out our grief.

Kent: Is this the promised end?
Edgar: Or image of that horror?
Albany: Fall, and cease.
                    act 5, scene 3, lines 255–62

Kent's rhetorical question implies a last judgment or apocalypse. Edgar's more imaginative variant embraces the entire play. Albany also beholds the world coming to an end.

Lear: This feather stirs, she lives: if it be so,
It is a chance which does redeem all sorrows
That ever I have felt.
Kent: O, my good master!
Lear: Prithee away!
Edgar: 'Tis noble Kent, your friend.
Lear: A plague upon you murderers, traitors all;
I might have saved her; now she's gone for ever.
Cordelia, Cordelia, stay a little. Ha?
What is't thou sayst? Her voice was ever soft,
Gentle, and low, an excellent thing in woman.
I killed the slave that was a-hanging thee.

In his giant agony, Lear is totally sane.

Gentleman: 'Tis true, my lords, he did.
Lear: Did I not, fellow?
I have seen the day, with my good biting falchion
I would have made them skip. I am old now
And these same crosses spoil me. [*to Kent*] Who are you?
Mine eyes are not o'the best, I'll tell you straight.
Kent: If Fortune brag of two she loved and hated,
One of them we behold.
Lear: This is a dull sight: are you not Kent?
Kent: The same;
Your servant Kent; where is your servant Caius?

156

Lear: He's a good fellow, I can tell you that;
He'll strike, and quickly too. He's dead and rotten.
Kent: No, my good lord, I am the very man—
Lear: I'll see that straight.
Kent: That from your first of difference and decay
Have followed your sad steps—
Lear: You're welcome hither.
Kent: Nor no man else. All's cheerless, dark and deadly;
Your eldest daughters have fordone themselves
And desperately are dead.
Lear: Ay, so I think.
Albany: He knows not what he says and vain is it
That we present us to him.
Edgar: Very bootless.

                    act 5, scene 3, lines 263–92

The great King is in shock, but knows well enough what he says.
His spirit centers totally upon his dead Cordelia.

Messenger: [*to Albany*] Edmund is dead, my lord.
Albany: That's but a trifle here.

And so it is. The death of Edmund has no meaning or value. The
iniquity of oblivion claims him.

Albany: You lords and noble friends, know our intent:
What comfort to this great decay may come
Shall be applied. For us, we will resign
During the life of this old majesty
To him our absolute power;

[*to Edgar and Kent*] you to your rights,
With boot and such addition as your honours
Have more than merited. All friends shall taste
The wages of their virtue and all foes
The cup of their deservings. O, see, see!

Albany vainly seeks a coherent future, but suddenly views Lear's burst of mistaken joy, as the King dies:

Lear: And my poor fool is hanged. No, no, no life!
Why should a dog, a horse, a rat, have life
And thou no breath at all? O thou'lt come no more,
Never, never, never, never, never.
Pray you undo this button. Thank you, sir. O, o, o, o.
Do you see this? Look on her: look, her lips,
Look there, look there!   *He dies.*

act 5, scene 3, lines 293–309

Hallucinating, Lear blends the identities of Cordelia and the Fool. The fivefold "never" is beyond the range of any actor I have heard. The King *sees* the resurrection of his child and expires in desperate joy.

Edgar: He faints: my lord, my lord!
Kent: Break, heart, I prithee break.
Edgar: Look up, my lord.
Kent: Vex not his ghost; O, let him pass. He hates him
That would upon the rack of this tough world
Stretch him out longer.

Edgar: O he is gone indeed.
Kent: The wonder is he hath endured so long;
He but usurped his life.

Edgar, unable to bear the loss of his godfather, battles the reality of Lear's death. Kent, with equal empathy, welcomes the liberation from suffering of his King.

Albany: Bear them from hence. Our present business
Is to general woe. [*to Kent and Edgar*] Friends of my soul, you
    twain,
Rule in this realm and the gored state sustain.

Why does Albany abdicate? Perhaps he feels the stigma of having fought against Lear and Cordelia, thus expediting Edmund's murderousness.

Kent: I have a journey, sir, shortly to go;
My master calls me, I must not say no.

Having served Lear in life, Kent desires only to follow him in and to death.

Edgar: The weight of this sad time we must obey,
Speak what we feel, not what we ought to say.
The oldest hath borne most; we that are young
Shall never see so much, nor live so long.
                Exeunt with a dead march.
                    act 5, scene 3, lines 310–25

Edgar inherits the ruined kingdom, casting aside the tradition of "the King is dead, long live the King." His troubled reign commences with this foreboding sense of brevity.

I write the final sentences of this book, wondering if all of us, like Lear, should cry that we are come unto this great stage of fools. Hamlet thought himself through to the truth that no man knew anything as he departed. Lear, suffering the woe and wonder of too much love, was bewildered by it, until he died.

ABOUT THE AUTHOR

Harold Bloom is Sterling Professor of Humanities at Yale University and a former Charles Eliot Norton Professor at Harvard. His more than forty books include *The Anxiety of Influence*, *The Western Canon*, *Shakespeare: The Invention of the Human*, *The American Religion*, *How to Read and Why*, *Stories and Poems for Extremely Intelligent Children of All Ages*, *The Daemon Knows*, *Falstaff: Give Me Life*, and *Cleopatra: I Am Fire and Air*. He is a member of the American Academy of Arts and Letters, a MacArthur Prize Fellow, and the recipient of many awards and honorary degrees, including the American Academy's Gold Medal for Belles Lettres and Criticism, the Hans Christian Andersen Award, the Catalonia International Prize, and the Alfonso Reyes International Prize of Mexico.